A-Z AYLESBURY

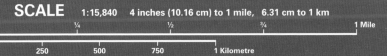

CONTE

Key to Map Pages	2-3	
Map Pages	4-33	

REFERENCE

A Road	A41	Church or Chapel	†
B Road	B4009	Cycleway (selected)	
Dual Carriageway		Fire Station	■
One-way Street Traffic flow on A roads is also indicated by a heavy line on the driver's left.		Hospital	🄷
		House Numbers (A & B Roads only)	15 3
Road Under Construction Opening dates are correct at the time of publication.		Information Centre	🄸
Proposed Road		National Grid Reference	480
		Police Station	▲
Restricted Access		Post Office	★
Pedestrianized Road		Safety Camera with Speed Limit Fixed cameras and long term road works cameras. Symbols do not indicate camera direction.	(30)
Track / Footpath			
Residential Walkway		Toilet:	
Railway	Heritage Station / Station / Tunnel / Level Crossing	without facilities for the Disabled	▽
		with facilities for the Disabled	▽
Built-up Area		Viewpoint	🔆
Local Authority Boundary		Educational Establishment	▭
Posttown Boundary		Hospital or Healthcare Building	▭
Postcode Boundary (within Posttown)		Industrial Building	▭
		Leisure or Recreational Facility	▭
		Place of Interest	▭
Map Continuation	12	Public Building	▭
		Shopping Centre or Market	▭
Car Park (selected)	P	Other Selected Buildings	▭

SCALE

1:15,840   4 inches (10.16 cm) to 1 mile,   6.31 cm to 1 km

0	¼	½	¾	1 Mile

0	250	500	750	1 Kilometre

Copyright of Geographers' A-Z Map Company Limited

Fairfield Road, Borough Green, Sevenoaks, Kent TN15 8PP
Telephone: 01732 781000 (Enquiries & Trade Sales)
01732 783422 (Retail Sales)
www.az.co.uk
Copyright © Geographers' A-Z Map Co. Ltd.
Edition 3 2012

 Ordnance Survey®
This product includes mapping data licensed from Ordnance Survey® with the permission of the Controller of Her Majesty's Stationery Office.

© Crown Copyright 2011. All rights reserved. Licence number 100017302

Safety camera information supplied by www.PocketGPSWorld.com
Speed Camera Location Database Copyright 2011 © PocketGPSWorld.com

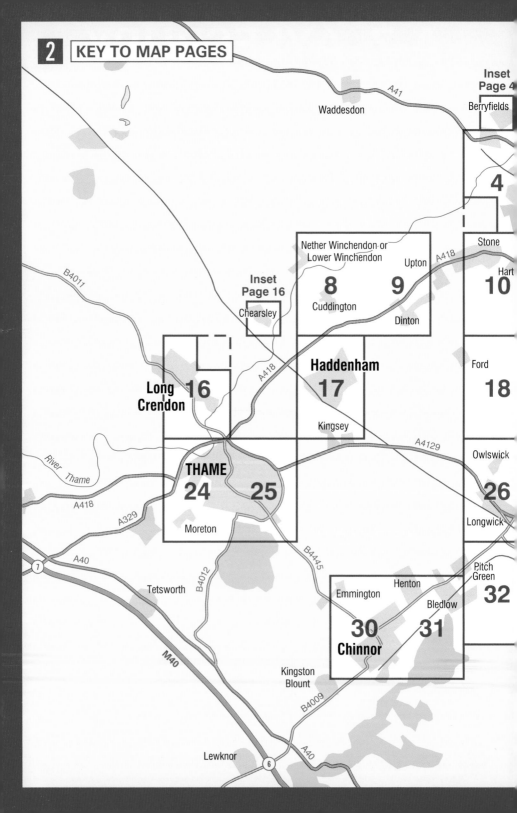

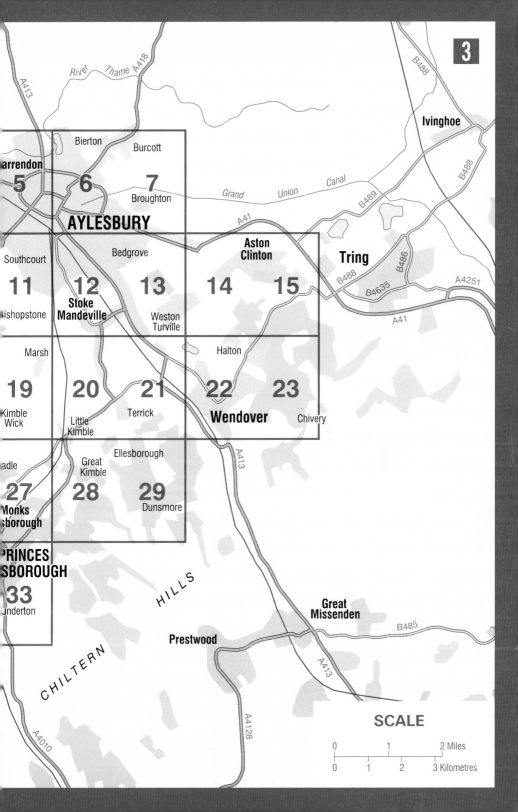

3

River Thame A418

A413

Bierton

Burcott

arrendon

5

6

7

Broughton

AYLESBURY

Ivinghoe

B488

B488

Grand Union Canal

B489

A41

Aston Clinton

Tring

B488

A4251

Southcourt

Bedgrove

11

12

13

14

15

Stoke Mandeville

ishopstone

Weston Turville

B4635

B486

A41

Marsh

Halton

19

20

21

22

23

Kimble Wick

Little Kimble

Terrick

Wendover

Chivery

adle

Ellesborough

Great Kimble

27

28

29

Monks sborough

Dunsmore

A413

PRINCES SBOROUGH

33

nderton

HILLS

Great Missenden

B485

Prestwood

A413

CHILTERN

A4128

A4010

SCALE

0   1   2 Miles

0   1   2   3 Kilometres

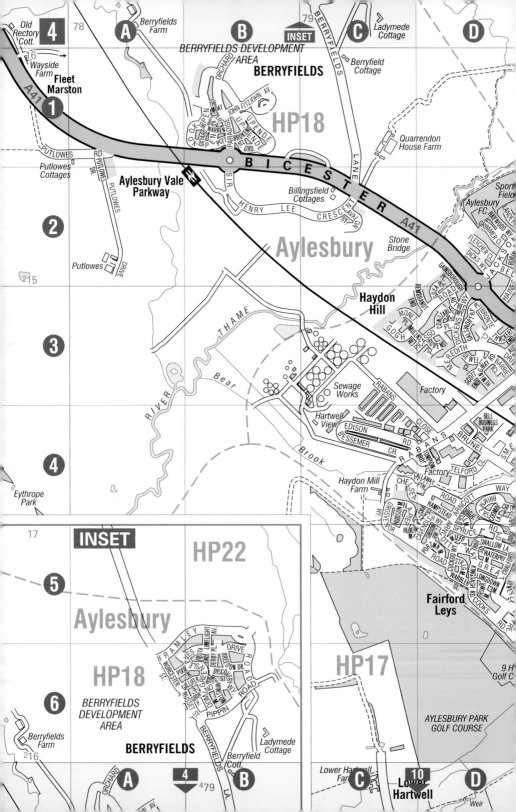

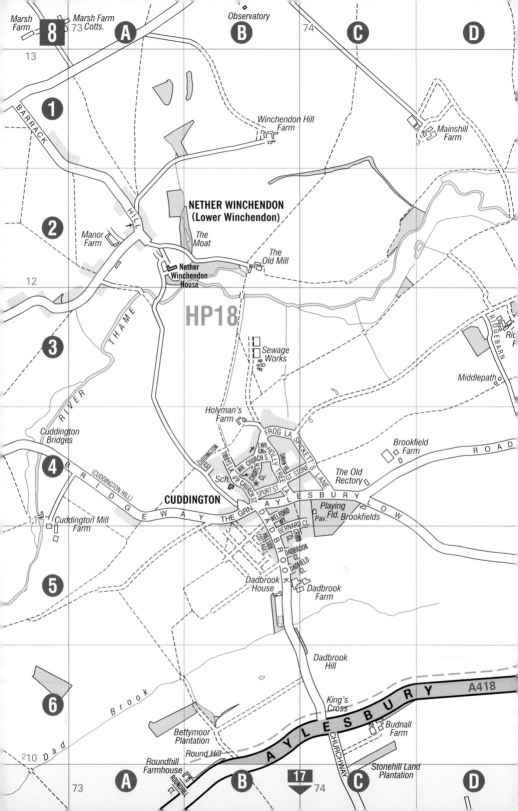

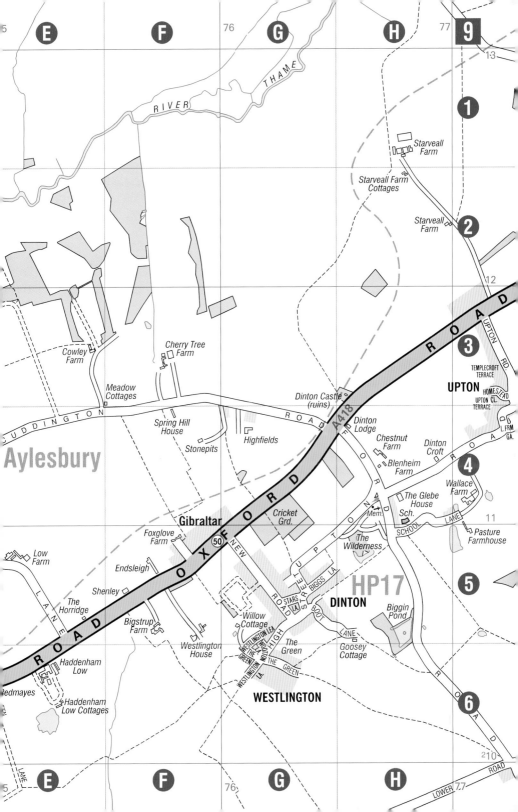

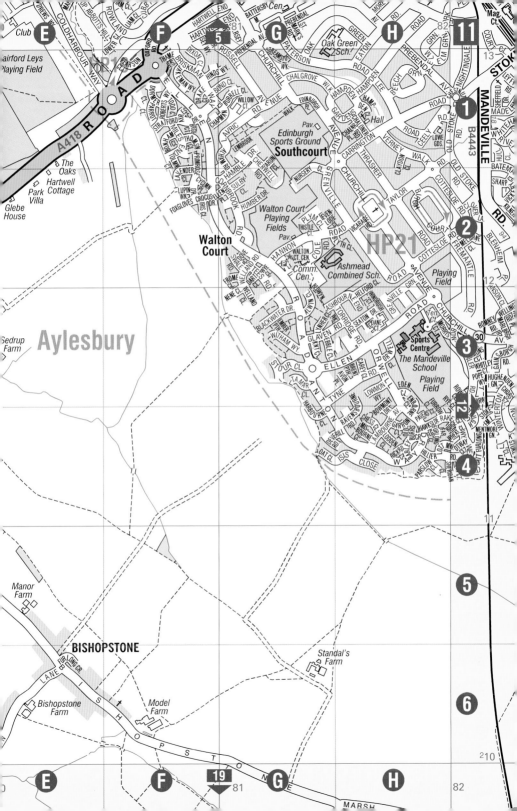

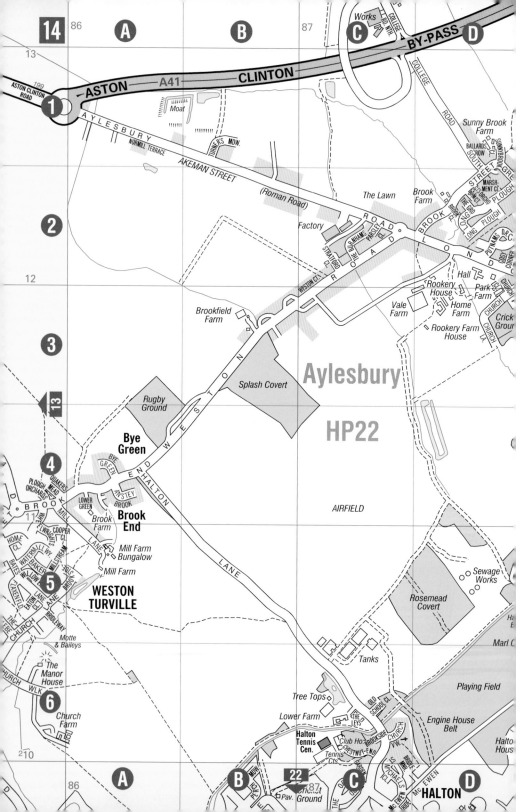

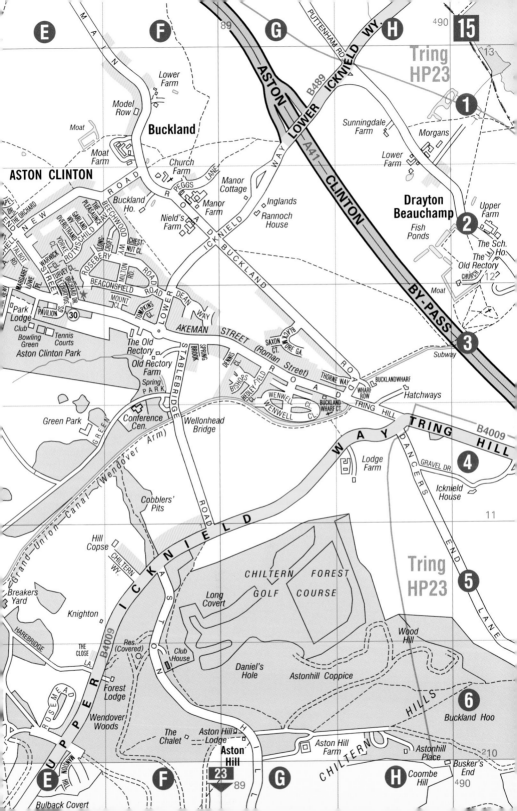

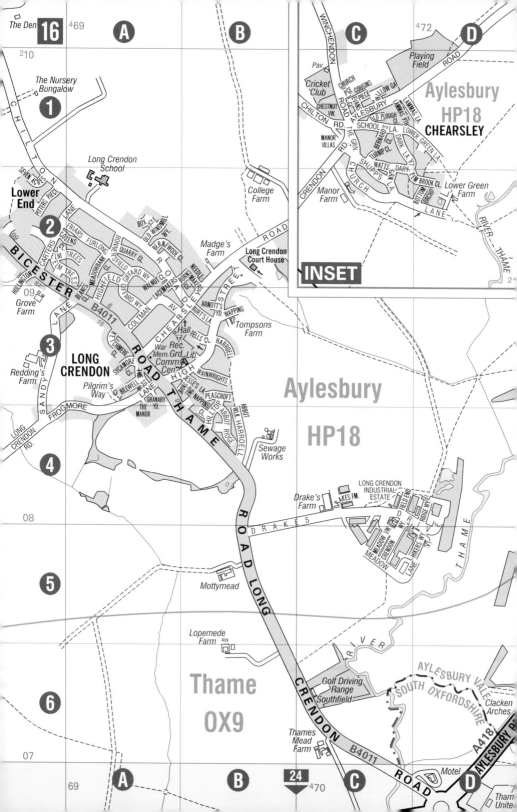

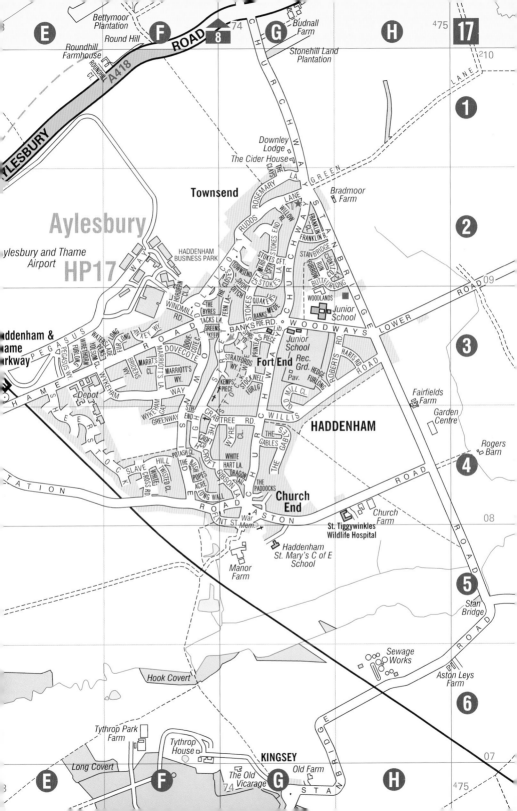

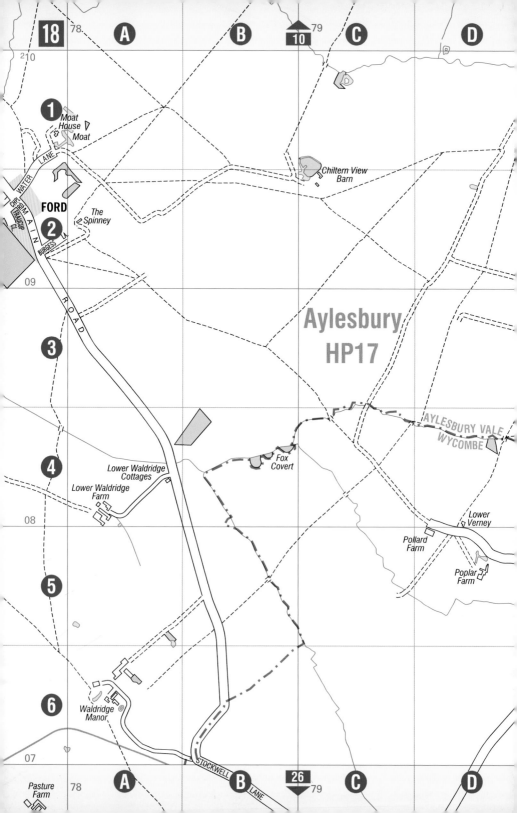

A   B   **10** 79   C   D

1 Moat House
Moat

Chiltern View
Barn

WATER LANE

CPL
HOLM
TRALLUP
CL

FORD

2

BURGESS LA

The Spinney

09

ROAD

3

Aylesbury
HP17

AYLESBURY VALE
WYCOMBE

Fox
Covert

4

Lower Waldridge
Cottages

Lower Waldridge
Farm

Lower
Verney

Pollard
Farm

08

Poplar
Farm

5

6

Waldridge
Manor

07

Pasture
Farm 78

STOCKWELL LANE

A   B   **26** 79   C   D

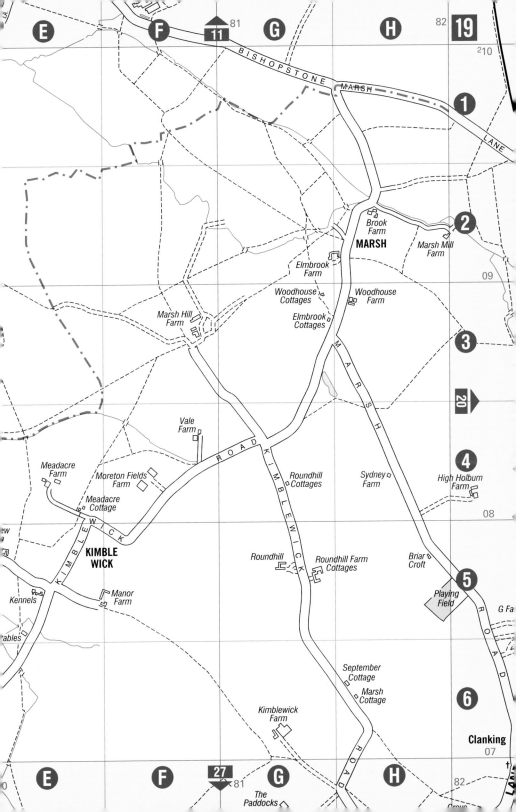

E   F   **11** 81   G   H   82   **19**   ²10

BISHOPSTONE MARSH LANE

1

Brook Farm

2

MARSH

Marsh Mill Farm

09

Elmbrook Farm

Woodhouse Cottages   Woodhouse Farm

Marsh Hill Farm   Elmbrook Cottages

3

MARSH

20

Vale Farm

4

Meadacre Farm   Moreton Fields Farm   Roundhill Cottages   Sydney Farm   High Holburn Farm

08

Meadacre Cottage

ROAD   KIMBLEWICK

ew

KIMBLE WICK

Roundhill   Roundhill Farm Cottages   Briar Croft

5

Kennels   Manor Farm

Playing Field

G Fa

ables

ROAD

September Cottage

Marsh Cottage

6

Kimblewick Farm

Clanking

07

E   F   **27** 81   G   H   82

The Paddocks

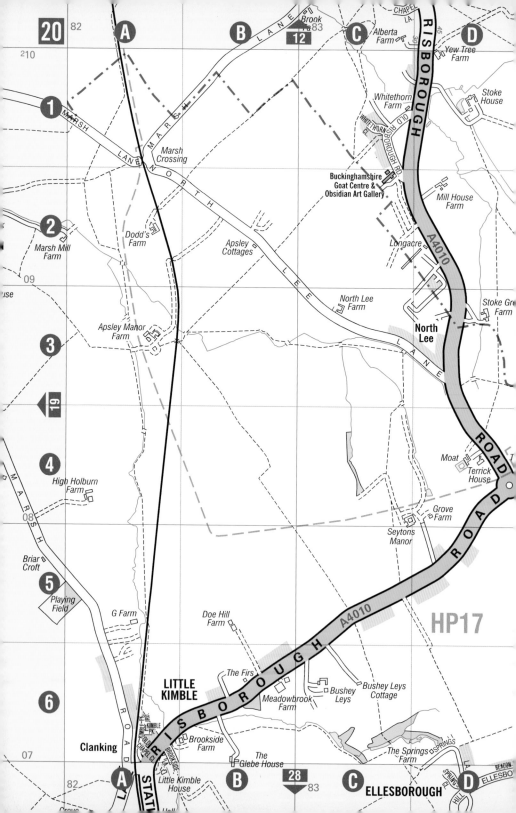

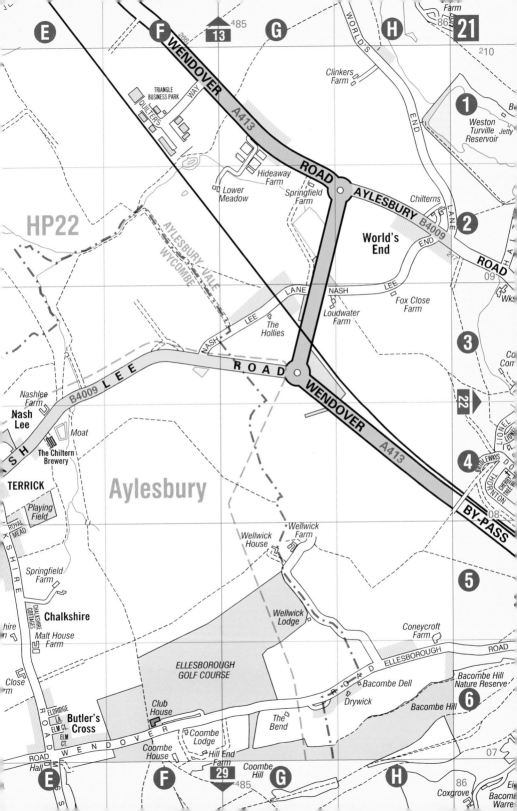

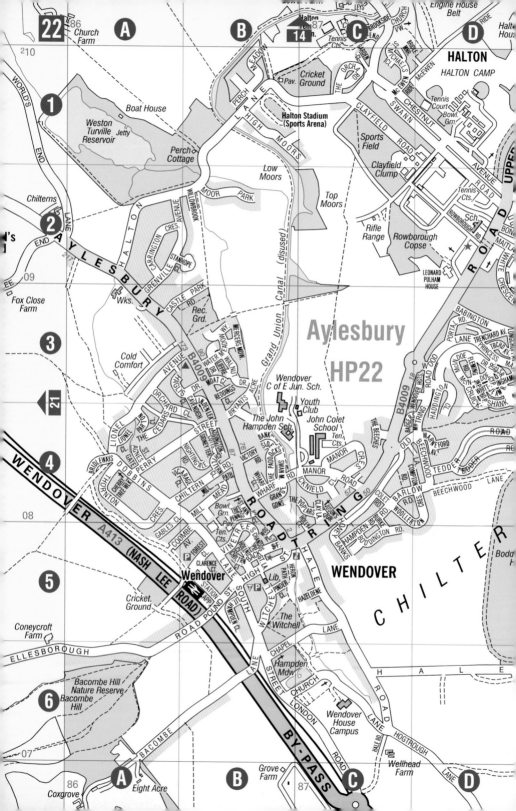

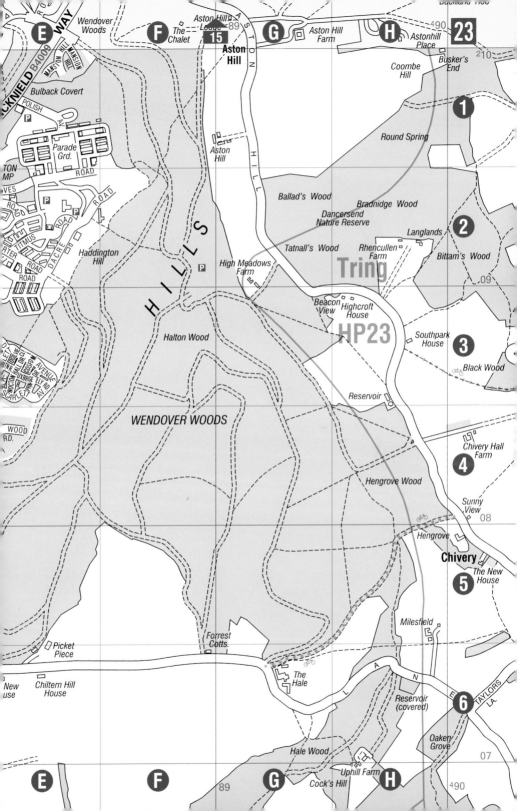

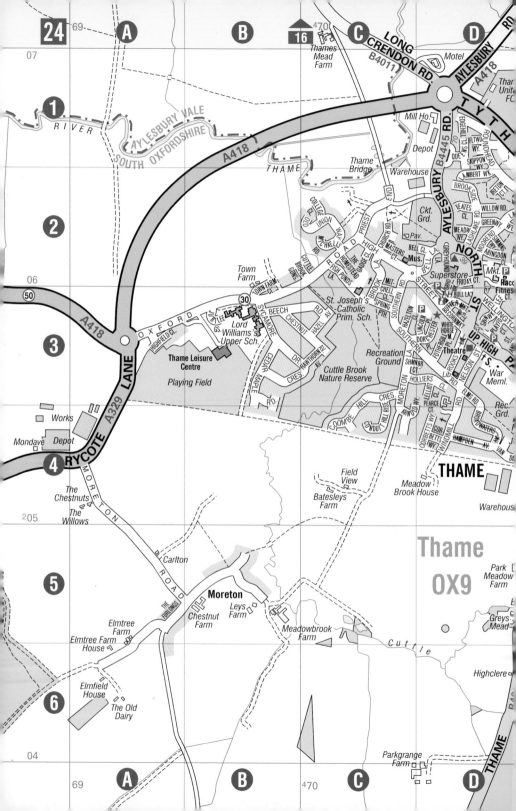

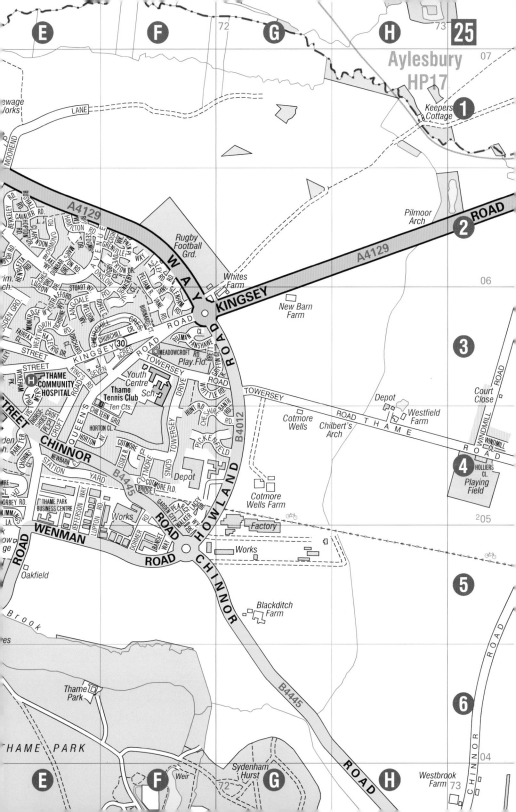

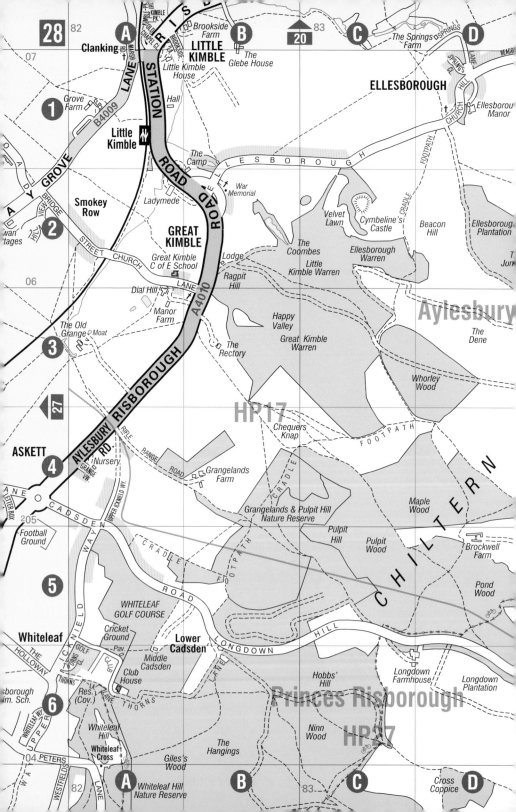

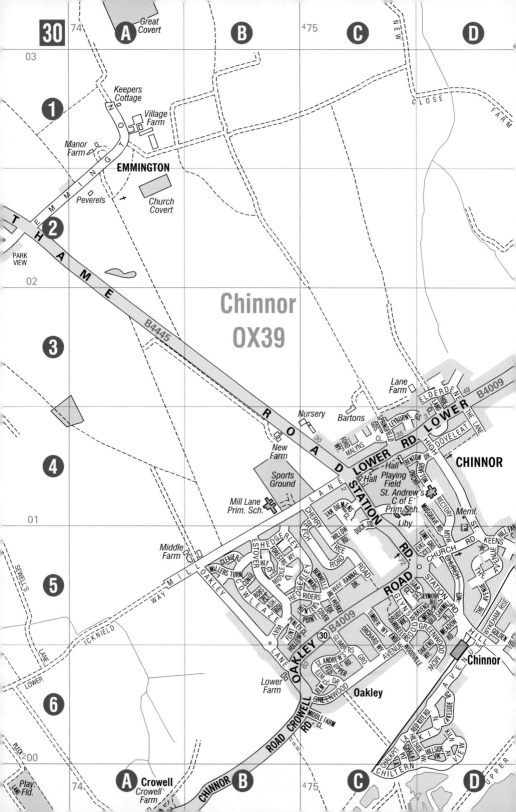

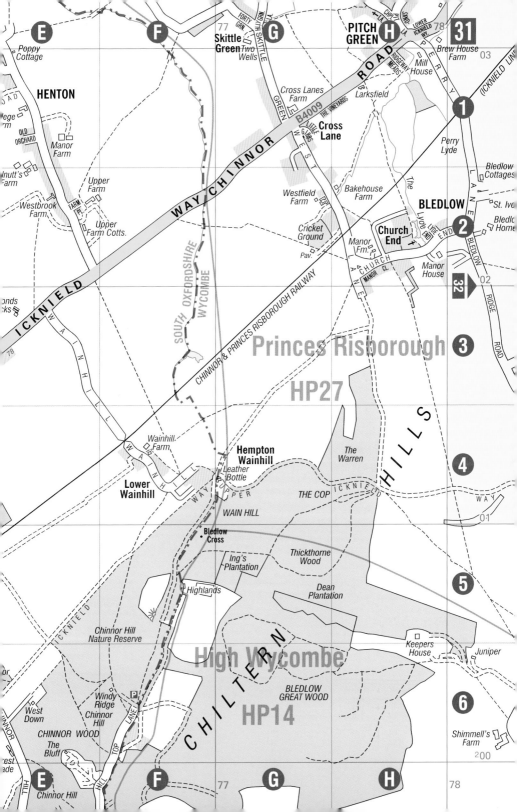

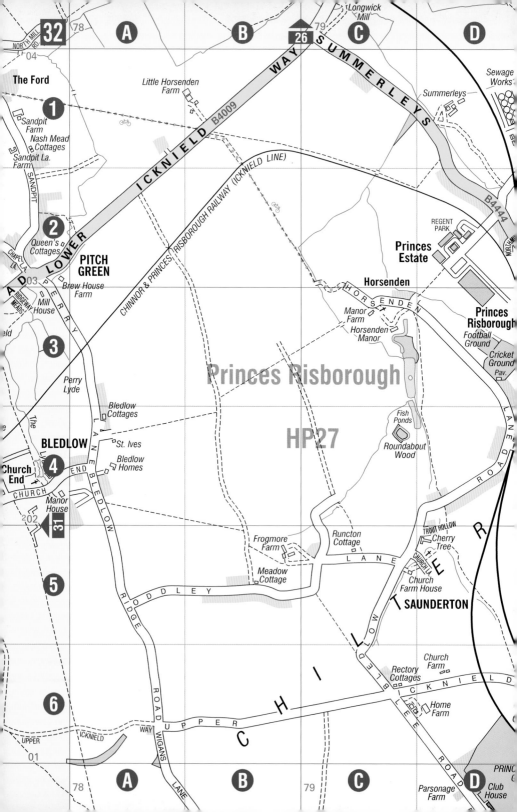

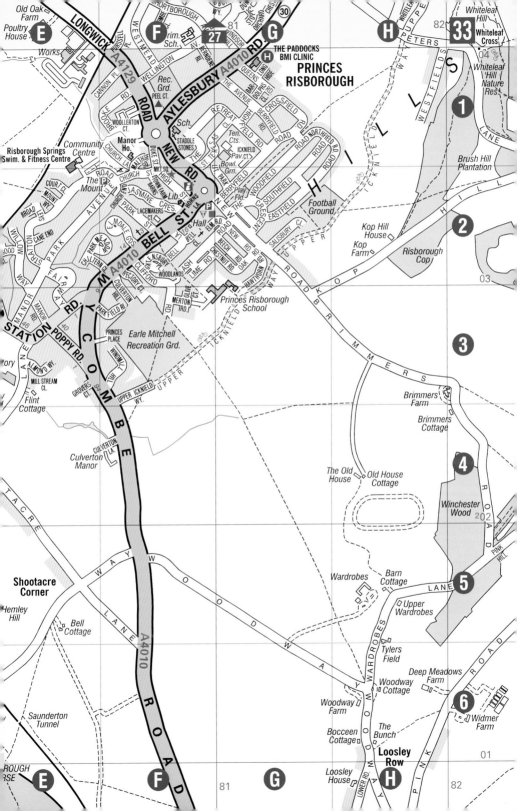

INDEX

Including Streets, Places & Areas, Hospitals etc., Industrial Estates,
Selected Flats & Walkways, Stations and Selected Places of Interest.

HOW TO USE THIS INDEX

1. Each street name is followed by its Postcode District, then by its Locality abbreviation(s) and then by its map reference;
e.g. **Abbey Rd.** HP19: Ayle . . . .3F **5** is in the HP19 Postcode District and the Aylesbury Locality and is to be found in square 3F on page **5**.
The page number is shown in bold type.

2. A strict alphabetical order is followed in which Av., Rd., St., etc. (though abbreviated) are read in full and as part of the street name;
e.g. **Elmdale Gdns.** appears after **Elm Ct.** but before **Elm Dr.**

3. Streets and a selection of flats and walkways that cannot be shown on the mapping, appear in the index with the thoroughfare to which they are connected
shown in brackets; e.g. **Archways** *HP20: Ayle* . . . .5H **5** (off Castle St.)

4. Addresses that are in more than one part are referred to as not continuous.

5. Places and areas are shown in the index in BLUE TYPE and the map reference is to the actual map square in which the town centre or area is located and not
to the place name shown on the map; e.g. AYLESBURY 5A **6**

6. An example of a selected place of interest is Buckinghamshire County Mus. 5H **5**

7. An example of a station is Aylesbury Station (Rail) . . . .6H **5**.

8. An example of a Hospital, Hospice or selected Healthcare facility is ROYAL BUCKINGHAMSHIRE HOSPITAL 4H **5**

GENERAL ABBREVIATIONS

All. : Alley	**Gt.** : Great	**Pk.** : Park
App. : Approach	**Grn.** : Green	**Pas.** : Passage
Av. : Avenue	**Gro.** : Grove	**Pl.** : Place
Bldgs. : Buildings	**Hgts.** : Heights	**Ri.** : Rise
Bus. : Business	**Ho.** : House	**Rd.** : Road
Cen. : Centre	**Ind.** : Industrial	**Shop.** : Shopping
Cl. : Close	**Info.** : Information	**Sth.** : South
Cnr. : Corner	**La.** : Lane	**Sq.** : Square
Cotts. : Cottages	**Lit.** : Little	**St.** : Street
Ct. : Court	**Lwr.** : Lower	**Ter.** : Terrace
Cres. : Crescent	**Mnr.** : Manor	**Up.** : Upper
Cft. : Croft	**Mkt.** : Market	**Va.** : Vale
Dr. : Drive	**Mdw.** : Meadow	**Vw.** : View
E. : East	**M.** : Mews	**Vs.** : Villas
Est. : Estate	**Mt.** : Mount	**Wlk.** : Walk
Fld. : Field	**Mus.** : Museum	**W.** : West
Gdns. : Gardens	**Nth.** : North	**Yd.** : Yard
Ga. : Gate	**Pde.** : Parade	

LOCALITY ABBREVIATIONS

Ask : **Askett**	Gt Kim : **Great Kimble**	Par H : **Parslows Hillock**
Ast C : **Aston Clinton**	Hadd : **Haddenham**	Prin R : **Princes Risborough**
Ayle : **Aylesbury**	Halt : **Halton**	St Leo : **St Leonards**
Bier : **Bierton**	Hart : **Hartwell**	Saun : **Saunderton**
Bish : **Bishopstone**	Hent : **Henton**	Sto M : **Stoke Mandeville**
Bled : **Bledlow**	Kim W : **Kimble Wick**	Sto : **Stone**
Bled R : **Bledlow Ridge**	King : **Kingsey**	Syde : **Sydenham**
Bro : **Broughton**	King B : **Kingston Blount**	Terr : **Terrick**
B'land : **Buckland**	L Grn : **Lacey Green**	Tha : **Thame**
But X : **Butlers Cross**	Lit K : **Little Kimble**	Tow : **Towersey**
Che : **Chearsley**	Long C : **Long Crendon**	Tring : **Tring**
Chin : **Chinnor**	Longw : **Longwick**	Upt : **Upton**
Crow : **Crowell**	Loos : **Loosely Row**	W'don : **Weedon**
Cudd : **Cuddington**	Mars : **Marsh**	Wend : **Wendover**
Dint : **Dinton**	Mead : **Meadle**	West T : **Weston Turville**
Dray B : **Drayton Beauchamp**	Mon R : **Monks Risborough**	Whit : **Whiteleaf**
Elle : **Ellesborough**	More : **Moreton**	Wils : **Wilstone**
Fleet M : **Fleet Marston**	Net W : **Nether Winchendon**	
Ford : **Ford**	Owls : **Owlswick**	

A

	Alham Rd. HP21: Ayle 1G **11**	Archer Dr. HP20: Ayle 3C **6**
	Allonby Way HP21: Ayle 6D **6**	Archive Cl. HP22: Ast C 2D **14**
	Almond Tree Dr. HP22: Sto M 3E **13**	Archways HP20: Ayle 5H **5**
	Almond Way HP27: Prin R 3E **33**	(off Castle St.)
Abbey Rd. HP19: Ayle 3F **5**	ALSCOT 6E **27**	Ardenham La. HP19: Ayle 4H **5**
Abbot Ridge HP18: Long C 4B **16**	Alscot La. HP27: Prin R 6E **27**	Ardenham St. HP19: Ayle 4G **5**
Abbots Way HP27: Mon R 6G **27**	Alton Ho. Office Pk. HP19: Ayle 4F **5**	Argyle Av. HP19: Ayle 3E **5**
Abbotts Cl. HP20: Ayle 4A **6**	Alwin Cl. HP21: Ayle 3G **11**	Arncott Way HP19: Ayle 4D **4**
Abbotts Rd. HP20: Ayle 4A **6**	Ambleside HP21: Ayle 2D **12**	Arnold Cl. HP22: Sto M 4E **13**
Abbot Wlk. HP18: Long C 4B **16**	Anchor La. HP20: Ayle 5A **6**	Arnold Ct. HP21: Ayle 1B **12**
Abingdon Cl. OX9: Tha 2D **24**	Andrews Way HP19: Ayle 6E **5**	Arnold Way OX9: Tha 4C **24**
Acres Way HP19: W'don 1G **5**	Anglo Bus. Pk. HP19: Ayle 4E **5**	Arnott's Yd. HP18: Long C 3B **16**
Addington Cotts. HP22: Wend 4B **22**	Angood Cl. HP27: Prin R 2E **33**	Arundel Grn. HP20: Ayle 3B **6**
Adkins Cl. HP19: Ayle 2D **4**	Angus Rd. HP19: Ayle 2E **5**	Asclough Cl. HP19: Ayle 2H **5**
Aidan Cl. HP22: Sto M 3C **12**	Anns Cl. HP21: Ayle 3C **12**	Ascott Cl. HP20: Ayle 4A **6**
Ailward Rd. HP19: Ayle 3D **4**	Anson Cl. HP21: Ayle 3A **12**	Ascott Rd. HP20: Ayle 4A **6**
Aiston Pl. HP20: Ayle 3B **6**	Anstey Brook HP22: West T 4A **14**	Ashbourne End HP21: Ayle 3G **11**
Albany Pl. HP19: Ayle 3E **5**	Anton Way HP21: Ayle 3G **11**	Ash Cl. HP20: Ayle 3C **6**
Albert St. HP20: Ayle 5C **6**	Anxey Way HP17: Hadd 3F **17**	Ashford Cl. HP21: Ayle 2C **12**
Albion St. HP20: Ayle 5A **6**	Aplin Rd. HP21: Ayle 1E **13**	Ash Gro. HP21: Ayle 6C **6**
Alder Rd. HP22: Sto M 3E **13**	Apsley Ct. HP19: Ayle 4H **5**	Ashley Row HP20: Ayle 4C **6**
Alderson Cl. HP19: Ayle 3E **5**	Aqua Vale Swimming & Fitness Cen. 5B **6**	Ashridge OX39: Chin 5B **30**
Alexander Rd. HP20: Ayle 4H **5**		

Ash Rd. HP27: Prin R 2F 33
ASKETT 4H 27
Askett La. HP27: Ask 4H 27
Askett Village La. HP27: Ask 3G 27
Aspen Cl. HP20: Ayle 3C 6
Astley Rd. OX9: Tha 2F 25
ASTON CLINTON 2E 5
Aston Clinton By-Pass
   HP22: Ast C, B'land . . . . .1A 14 & 1G 15
Aston Clinton Rd. HP22: West T 6F 7
Aston Cl. HP19: Ayle 2E 5
ASTON HILL 6G 15
Aston Hill HP22: Halt 5F 15
Aston Rd. HP17: Hadd 4G 17
Astronomy Way HP19: Ayle 5E 5
      (off Queensgate)
Austen Pl. HP19: Ayle 3D 4
Autumn Cl. HP19: Ayle 2E 5
Avalon St. HP18: Ayle 2C 4
Avenue, The HP27: Prin R 1G 33
   OX39: Chin .5D 30
Avocet Way HP19: Ayle 2A 6
Avon Pl. HP21: Ayle 3H 11
AYLESBURY 5A 6
Aylesbury Bus. Cen. HP19: Ayle 4F 5
Aylesbury College Sports Cen. 6G 5
Aylesbury Golf Course 1F 7
Aylesbury Pk. Golf Course 6E 5
Aylesbury Rd. HP17: Dint, Hadd 1E 17
   HP18: Che 1C 16
   HP18: Cudd .4B 8
   HP22: Ast C .1A 14
   HP22: Wend .2H 21
   HP27: Ask, Mon R, Prin R 1F 33
   OX9: Hadd, Tha 2D 24
Aylesbury Shop. Cen. HP20: Ayle 4A 6
Aylesbury Station (Rail) 6H 5
Aylesbury Vale Parkway Station (Rail) . . .2B 4
Ayleswater HP19: Ayle 1A 6
Ayres Cl. HP21: Ayle 1F 11
Ayrshire Cl. HP19: Ayle 2E 5

B

Babington Rd. HP22: Halt 3D 22
Back St. HP22: Wend 5B 22
Bacombe Hill Nature Reserve 6A 22
Bacombe La. HP22: Wend 6A 22
Badgers Mdw. HP22: Halt 4C 22
Badgers Ri. HP17: Sto 2A 10
Badrick Rd. HP19: Ayle 3D 4
Baird Pl. HP22: Halt 3D 22
Bakers Wlk. HP22: West T 5H 13
Balfore Ter. HP19: Ayle 3F 5
      (off Holland Rd.)
Balfour Way HP20: Ayle 3A 6
Ballard Cl. HP21: Ayle 2D 12
Ballards Row HP22: Ast C 1D 14
Bandet Way OX9: Tha 5F 25
Bankside HP22: Wend 4B 22
Banks Pde. HP17: Hadd 3G 17
Banks Rd. HP17: Hadd 3G 17
Bannister Rd. OX9: Tha 3G 25
Bardolphs Cl. HP27: Prin R 1G 33
Bardon Grn. HP20: Ayle 3A 6
Bar La. HP27: Longw, Owls 4B 26
Barley Cl. HP22: West T 5H 13
Barley Cres. HP21: Ayle 4H 11
Barlow Rd. HP22: Wend 4C 22
Barnard Cres. HP21: Ayle 2B 12
Barnett Way HP22: Bier 1D 6
Barn Rd. HP27: Longw 5B 26
Barnsbury Av. HP20: Ayle 5D 6
Barnshaw Ho. HP21: Ayle 6H 5
Barrack Hill HP18: Net W 1A 8
Barrie Cl. HP19: Ayle 3D 4
Base Cl. HP20: Ayle 3C 6
Batchelor Cl. HP20: Ayle 3B 6
Bateman Dr. HP21: Ayle 1A 12
Bates Cl. HP20: Ayle 3B 6
Bates La. HP22: West T 5H 13
Battersby M. HP21: Ayle 6G 5
Batt Furlong HP21: Ayle 4A 12
Battle Mdw. HP19: Ayle 2G 5
Baynton Rd. HP22: Wend 3A 12
Beacon Cl. HP17: Sto 2A 10
Beaconsfield Rd. HP21: Ayle 6A 6
   HP22: Ast C .2E 15
Beacon Vw. HP17: Elle 1D 28
Bearbrook Cl. HP21: Ayle 6G 5
Beaufort Cl. HP21: Ayle 6F 7
Beckett Cl. HP19: Ayle 3E 5

BEDGROVE 1D 12
Bedgrove HP21: Ayle 1E 13
Bedgrove Ho. HP21: Ayle 2A 12
Bedlington M. HP19: Ayle 5C 4
Bedwyn Wlk. HP21: Ayle 3G 11
Beech Cl. HP22: Bier 2D 6
Beeches, The HP22: Wend 4C 22
Beech Grn. HP21: Ayle 1H 11
Beech Rd. HP27: Prin R 2G 33
   OX9: Tha 3B 24
   OX39: Chin .5C 30
Beechwood Ho. HP22: Ast C 2F 15
      (off Beechwood Way)
Beechwood La.
   HP22: Wend, Halt 4D 22
Beechwood Way HP22: Ast C 2F 15
Beeston La. HP19: W'don 1F 5
Belgrave Rd. HP19: Ayle 2D 4
Bell Bus. Pk. HP19: Ayle 4D 4
Bell Cl. HP27: Prin R 2F 33
   OX9: Tha 2D 24
Bell Cres. HP27: Longw 5C 26
Belle Vue HP17: Sto 2A 10
Bell La. HP27: Prin R 2F 33
   OX9: Tha 2D 24
Bell St. HP27: Prin R 2F 33
Benton Dr. OX39: Chin 4C 30
Benwells OX39: Chin 5C 30
Beresford Av. HP19: Ayle 2G 5
Berkeley Ri. HP19: Ayle 3F 5
Berkeley Rd. OX9: Tha 2E 25
Bernard Cl. HP18: Cudd 5B 8
Bernard's Cl. HP18: Che 1C 16
Bernewode Ri. HP27: Prin R 1F 33
Bernewode Cl. HP18: Long C 2A 16
Berryfield Rd. HP19: Ayle 2F 5
   HP27: Prin R 1G 33
BERRYFIELDS . . . . .6B 4 & 1B 4
Berryfields Development Area
   HP18: Ayle . . . . .6A 4 & 1B 4
Berryfields La. HP18: Ayle 6B 4
Bessemer Cres. HP19: Ayle 4C 4
Bicester Rd. HP18: Ayle 1B 4
   HP18: Long C 2A 16
   HP19: Ayle 1B 4
BIERTON 2D 6
Bierton Rd. HP20: Ayle 4A 6
Bierton Sports Cen. 2E 7
Biggs La. HP17: Dint 5G 9
Billwell HP18: Long C 3A 16
Birch Ct. HP21: Ayle 2H 11
Bishops Fld. HP22: Ast C 3G 15
Bishops Mdw. HP22: Bier 2C 6
BISHOPSTONE 6E 11
Bishopstone HP17: Bish, Sto 4C 10
Bishopstone Rd. HP17: Sto 2A 10
Bishops Wlk. HP21: Ayle 1B 12
Bittenham Cl. HP17: Sto 3C 10
Bittern Way HP21: Ayle 2A 6
Blackmore Cl. OX9: Tha 4E 25
Blackmore Ga. HP22: B'land 3G 15
Blacksmiths HP27: Longw 4B 26
Blackwater Dr. HP21: Ayle 3G 11
Blake St. HP21: Ayle 4G 5
Blake Way OX9: Tha 2E 25
Blanchard Ter. HP19: Ayle 3F 5
      (off Holland Rd.)
Blanes Cl. HP18: Long C 3A 16
BLEDLOW 4A 32
Bledlow Cross .5F 31
Bledlow Ridge Rd. HP27: Bled 4A 32
Bledlow Rd. HP27: Saun 6C 32
Blenheim Cl. HP27: Longw 4B 26
Blenheim Pl. HP21: Ayle 2A 12
Blyth Cl. HP21: Ayle 2H 11
Boddington Rd. HP22: Wend 5C 22
Bodiam Cl. HP21: Ayle 2D 12
Bond Cl. HP21: Ayle 1G 11
Bonham Carter Rd. HP22: Halt 2D 22
Bonham Cl. HP21: Ayle 1F 11
Bonham Ct. HP22: Ast C 2D 14
Bonnersfield HP18: Long C 2A 16
Boot La. HP17: Dint 5G 9
Bottom Orchard HP18: Che 3B 16
Bourbon St. HP20: Ayle 5H 5
Bowerbank Ct. HP20: Ayle 4A 6
Bowler Rd. HP21: Ayle 4A 12
Bowmont Dr. HP21: Ayle 4H 11
Boxer Rd. HP27: Longw 5C 26
Bracken Way HP21: Ayle 6F 5
Braddenham Wlk. HP21: Ayle 3A 12
Braddens Furlong
   HP18: Long C 3B 16
Braden Cl. HP21: Ayle 1C 12

Brambling HP19: Ayle 2A 6
Bramcote Cl. HP20: Ayle 5E 7
Bramley Rd. HP18: Ayle 6A 4
Breedon Dr. HP18: Ayle 6B 4
Brent Path HP21: Ayle 3H 11
Brentwood Way HP21: Ayle 1D 12
Brett Cl. OX9: Tha 3F 25
Briars Cl. HP19: Ayle 3F 5
Brick Kiln La. HP22: Bier 1E 7
Bridens Way HP17: Hadd 3F 17
Bridgegate Bus. Pk. HP19: Ayle 4F 5
Bridge St. HP17: Gt Kim 2H 27
Bridge Ter. OX9: Tha 4F 25
Bridgeway HP18: Che, Cudd 4A 8
Bridgeways HP22: Halt 6C 14
Bridleway HP27: Prin R 3G 33
Bridleways HP22: Wend 4A 22
Brimmers Rd. HP27: Prin R 3G 33
Brimmers Way HP19: Ayle 4D 4
Brimstone La. HP19: W'don 1G 5
Briskman Way HP21: Ayle 1F 11
Britannia St. HP20: Ayle 5A 6
Britannia Wlk. HP20: Ayle 5A 6
Broadfields HP19: Ayle 4E 5
Broadfields Ct. HP19: Ayle 4E 5
Broadfields Retail Pk.
   HP19: Ayle 3E 5
Broad Leys HP27: Prin R 2E 33
Broadwaters Av. OX9: Tha 4D 24
Brokend HP18: Ayle 1B 4
Brompton Cl. HP19: Ayle 3F 5
Brompton Cres. HP19: Ayle 3F 5
Bronte Cl. HP19: Ayle 3D 4
Brook Cl. HP22: Ast C 2D 14
BROOK END 4A 14
Brook End HP22: West T 4H 13
Brooke Rd. HP27: Prin R 1F 33
Brook La. OX9: Tha 3C 24
Brookside HP22: Halt 6C 14
   HP22: West T 5H 13
   OX9: Tha 2D 24
Brookside La. HP17: Lit K 6A 20
Brookside Ter. HP21: Ayle 5A 6
      (off Highbridge Wlk.)
Brook St. HP22: Ast C 2D 14
Brotheridge Ct. HP21: Ayle 1F 11
BROUGHTON .5E 7
Broughton Av. HP20: Ayle 5D 6
Broughton Cl. HP22: Bier 2D 6
Broughton Crossing HP22: Bro 3E 7
Broughton La. HP22: Ayle 4E 7
   HP22: Bier, Bro 2E 7
      (not continuous)
Brudenell Dr. HP22: Sto M 6D 2
Brunel Rd. HP19: Ayle 4D 4
Brunswick Cl. HP19: Ayle 2E 5
Bryanston Av. HP20: Ayle 3B 6
Bryants Acre HP22: Wend 4B 22
Buckingham Ct. HP19: Ayle 4H 5
      (off Buckingham St.)
Buckingham Rd. HP19: Ayle, W'don 1H 5
Buckinghamshire County Mus. 5H 5
Buckinghamshire Goat Cen. &
   Obsidian Art Gallery 2C 20
BUCKLAND 1F 15
Buckland Rd. HP22: B'land 2G 15
Bucklandwharf HP22: B'land 3H 15
Buckland Wharf Ct. HP22: Ast C 3G 15
Bullfinch Gdns. HP19: Ayle 2B 6
Bull La. OX9: Tha 3D 24
BURCOTT 2E 7
Burcott Cl. HP22: Bier 2D 6
Burcott La. HP22: Bier 1E 7
Burgess La. HP17: Ford 2A 18
Burke Rd. HP22: Wend 4C 22
Burnards Ct. OX9: Tha 3F 25
Burnhams, The HP22: Ast C 2C 14
Burnhams Fld. HP22: West T 1G 13
Burns Cl. HP18: Long C 2B 16
Burns Ct. HP21: Ayle 1B 12
Burrell Ct. HP21: Ayle 1G 11
Bursars Path HP19: Ayle 1G 5
      (off Charles Pym Rd.)
Burton La. HP27: Mon R 6G 27
Burt's La. HP18: Long C 3B 16
Bush, The HP17: Hadd 4F 17
BUTLER'S CROSS 6E 21
Butler Wlk. HP19: Ayle 6E 5
Butter Mkt. OX9: Tha 3D 24
Buttermere HP21: Ayle 6D 6
Buttlurlong HP17: Hadd 2G 17
BYE GREEN 4A 14
Bye Grn. HP22: West T 4A 14

C

Byres, The. HP17: Hadd 3F 17
Byron Rd. HP21: Ayle 1B 12

Cade Pl. HP22: Halt 3E 23
Cadsden Rd. HP27: Whit 4H 27
Caldicot Cl. HP21: Ayle 1D 12
CALIFORNIA 6H 5
California HP21: Ayle 6H 5
(off Penn Rd.)
Callaway Path HP19: Ayle 4D 4
Camborne Av. HP21: Ayle 2C 12
Cambridge Cl. HP20: Ayle 4A 6
(not continuous)
Cambridge Pl. HP20: Ayle 5H 5
Cambridge St. HP20: Ayle 5H 5
Cam Mead HP21: Ayle 1D 12
Campion Cl. HP20: Ayle 5E 7
Canal Side Ter. HP21: Ayle 5H 5
(off Highbridge Rd.)
Cane End HP27: Prin R 2E 33
Canford Cl. HP21: Ayle 2B 12
Cannock Rd. HP20: Ayle 2H 5
Cannon Pl. HP27: Prin R 1F 33
Canterbury Cl. HP27: Mon R 6F 27
Cantley Cl. HP20: Ayle 3A 6
Carbine Path HP19: Ayle 1H 5
Carey Cl. HP21: Ayle 3H 11
Carlton Cl. HP19: Ayle 3E 5
Carlton Ct. HP27: Prin R 2F 33
(off Bell St.)
Carlyle Av. HP21: Ayle 1A 12
Carnation Way HP21: Ayle 2A 12
Carr Cl. HP19: Ayle 3E 5
Carrington Cres. HP22: Wend 2A 22
Carrington Rd. HP21: Ayle 1H 11
Carters La. HP18: Long C 2A 16
Carters Ride HP22: Sto M 5D 12
Castle Cl. HP20: Ayle 5H 5
(off Castle St.)
Castle Ct. HP20: Ayle 5H 5
(off Castle St.)
Castlefields HP22: Sto M 4E 13
Castle Pk. Rd. HP22: Wend 3A 22
Castle St. HP20: Ayle 5H 5
Caudery Pl. HP22: Halt 3D 22
Cavalier Rd. OX9: Tha 2E 25
Cavalry Path HP19: Ayle 2H 5
(off Nugent Cl.)
Cavendish Cl. HP22: Wend 3B 22
Cavendish Wlk. OX9: Tha 2F 25
Cavendish Way HP19: Ayle 5D 4
Caversham Grn. HP20: Ayle 4H 5
Cedar Cl. HP20: Ayle 3C 6
Cedar Cres. OX9: Tha 3B 24
Cedars, The HP22: Wend 4A 22
Ceely Rd. HP21: Ayle 1H 11
Centenary Cotts. HP27: Longw 4B 26
Centre Pde. HP27: Mon R 6F 27
Chadbone Cl. HP20: Ayle 5H 5
Chadwell Path HP21: Ayle 1E 13
(off Long Meadow)
Chaffinch HP19: Ayle 1B 6
Chairmakers Cl. HP27: Prin R 4E 33
Chalford Way HP19: Ayle 5D 4
Chalgrove End HP22: Sto M 5D 12
Chalgrove Rd. OX9: Tha 2E 25
Chalgrove Wlk. HP21: Ayle 1G 11
Chalkhill Blue Cl. HP19: W'don 1G 5
Chalkpit La. OX39: Chin 6C 30
CHALKSHIRE 5E 21
Chalkshire Cotts. HP17: But X 5E 21
Chalkshire Rd. HP17: But X, Terr 4E 21
Chaloner Pl. HP21: Ayle 1H 11
Chaloner Rd. HP21: Ayle 1H 11
Chamberlain Rd. HP19: Ayle 4F 5
Chancellors Rd. HP19: W'don 1G 5
Chandos Pl. HP22: Wend 5B 22
Chantry, The HP20: Ayle 5H 5
(off Church St.)
Chantry Rd. HP19: Ayle 2G 5
Chapel Dr. HP22: Ast C 2E 15
Chapel La. HP22: Sto M 6C 12
HP22: Wend 6B 22
HP27: Bled 1H 31
Chapel Rd. HP17: Ford 2A 18
Chapman Cl. HP21: Ayle 1F 11
Charles Cl. HP21: Ayle 3D 12
Charles Dr. OX9: Tha 2E 25
Charles Pym Rd. HP19: Ayle 1G 5
Charmfield Rd. HP21: Ayle 2C 12
Chaucer Pl. HP21: Ayle 1A 12

Chaundler Dr. HP19: W'don 1F 5
CHEARSLEY 1C 16
Chearsley Rd. HP18: Long C 3A 16
Chelsea Rd. HP19: Ayle 4C 4
Cheney Wlk. HP20: Ayle 3B 6
(off Cheney Way)
Cheney Way HP20: Ayle 3B 6
Chequers Ct. HP21: Ayle 3A 12
Cherry Tree Rd. OX39: Chin 4C 30
Cherry Tree Wlk.
HP22: Wend 4A 22
Cherwell Rd. HP21: Ayle 1G 11
Cheshire Rd. OX9: Tha 4F 25
Chess Cl. HP21: Ayle 4H 11
Chesterfield Cl. HP17: Sto 2A 10
Chesterfield Pl. HP19: Ayle 5F 5
Chestnut Av. HP22: Halt 1C 22
OX9: Tha .3B 24
Chestnut Cl. HP22: Ast C 2F 15
HP27: Mon R 6G 27
Chestnut Cres. HP21: Ayle 1A 12
Chestnut End HP22: Halt 6C 14
Chestnut Rd. HP27: Prin R 2F 33
Chestnut Vw. HP18: Che 1C 16
Chestnut Way HP22: Sto M 6C 12
HP27: Longw 5C 26
Chiltern Av. HP17: Sto 2B 10
Chiltern Brewery, The 4E 21
Chiltern Cl. HP17: Sto 2B 10
HP22: Wend 4B 22
HP27: Prin R 2E 33
Chiltern Ct. HP22: Wend 5B 22
Chiltern Forest Golf Course 6F 15
Chiltern Gro. OX9: Tha 4E 25
Chiltern Rd. HP22: Wend 4B 22
Chiltern St. HP21: Ayle 1A 12
Chiltern Vw. HP17: Sto 3B 10
OX39: Chin 6C 30
Chiltern Way HP22: Ast C 5F 15
Chilton Pl. HP20: Ayle 4A 6
Chilton Rd. HP18: Che 1C 16
HP18: Long C 1A 16
CHINNOR 5D 30
Chinnor & Princes Risborough Railway
Chinnor Station 6D 30
Chinnor Hill OX39: Chin 6E 31
Chinnor Hill Nature Reserve 5F 31
Chinnor Rd. HP27: Bled 2G 31
OX9: Tha, Tow . . . . . . .4E 25 & 6H 25
OX39: Crow, King B 6B 30
CHIVERY 5H 23
Chowns Cl. OX9: Tha 4E 25
Church Cl. HP18: Cudd 4B 8
HP22: Ast C 2D 14
Church Ct. HP22: Sto M 5D 12
CHURCH END
HP17 . . . . .4G 17
HP27 . . . . .2H 31
Church End HP27: Bled 2H 31
HP27: Prin R 2F 33
Church Farm Cl. HP22: Bier 2C 6
Church Hill HP17: Elle 1D 28
Churchill Av. HP21: Ayle 6G 5
Churchill Ct. HP21: Ayle 6A 6
(off Beaconsfield Rd.)
Churchill Cres. OX9: Tha 3E 25
Church La. HP17: Gt Kim 2A 28
HP18: Che 2C 16
HP22: Ast C 3D 14
HP22: Dray B 2H 15
HP22: Wend 6B 22
HP22: West T 6H 13
HP27: Prin R 1F 33
HP27: Saun 5D 32
OX39: Chin 5D 30
Churchmere Wlk. HP21: Ayle 1G 11
(off Hamble Dr.)
Church Piece HP18: Che 1C 16
Church Rd. OX9: Tha 2C 24
OX39: Chin 5D 30
Church St. HP20: Ayle 5H 5
Church Vw. HP22: Halt 6C 14
Church Wlk. HP22: West T 6H 13
Church Way HP17: Sto 2A 10
Churchway HP17: Hadd 6C 8
CLANKING 1A 28
Claremont Cl. HP21: Ayle 2B 12
Clarence Ct. HP22: Wend 5B 22
Clarendon Dr. OX9: Tha 2E 25
Clarke Ct. HP20: Ayle 3B 6
Clarke Wlk. HP20: Ayle 3B 6
(off Clarke Ct.)
Claydon Cl. HP21: Ayle 1H 11

Claydons Path HP21: Ayle 4A 12
Claydons Pl. HP27: Longw 4B 26
Clayfield Rd. HP22: Halt 1C 22
Clay La. HP22: Wend 4C 22
Clays, The HP17: Hadd 2G 17
Cleavers OX39: Chin 5B 30
Cleveland Pk. HP20: Ayle 2B 6
Cleveland Pl. HP20: Ayle 3B 6
(off Cleveland Pk.)
Cleveland Rd. HP20: Ayle 2A 6
Clifford Rd. HP27: Prin R 2F 33
Clifton Bus. Pk. HP19: Ayle 4E 5
Clifton Grn. HP19: Ayle 3F 5
Clinton Cres. HP21: Ayle 5C 6
Clivedon HP19: W'don 1H 5
Cloisters, The HP20: Ayle 5H 5
(off Gt. Western St.)
Close, The HP22: Bier 1C 6
HP22: Halt 6E 15
Closes, The HP17: Hadd 3G 17
Clouded Yellow Path HP19: W'don 1F 5
Clover La. HP19: Ayle 2A 12
Cock La. HP20: Ayle 4H 5
(shown as Lucky La.)
Coldharbour Way HP19: Ayle 4E 5
Cole Rd. HP21: Ayle 2G 11
Colet Rd. HP22: Wend 4C 22
College Cl. OX9: Tha 2C 24
College Rd. Nth. HP22: Ast C 1C 14
College Rd. Sth. HP22: Ast C 1D 14
Colonel Grantham Av. HP19: Ayle, W'don . . .1G 5
Coltman Av. HP18: Long C 3A 16
Comfrey, The HP19: Ayle 1A 6
Como Rd. HP20: Ayle 5D 6
Compton Rd. HP22: Wend 4C 22
Conduit Hill Ri. OX9: Tha 4C 24
Conigre OX39: Chin 5B 30
Coniston Grn. HP20: Ayle 2H 5
Connaught Rd. HP20: Ayle 5E 7
Conspec Ho. HP19: Ayle 4G 5
Constable Pl. HP19: Ayle 3D 4
Conway Cl. HP21: Ayle 6B 6
Cooks Rd. HP19: Ayle 5D 4
COOMBE 2E 29
Coombe Av. HP22: Wend 5A 22
Coombe Cl. HP22: Sto M 5E 13
Coombe Hill Cres. OX9: Tha 4C 24
Coombe Hill Monument 1F 29
Coombe La. HP20: Ayle 4D 4
Cooper's Yd. HP20: Ayle 4H 5
Coppice Cl. HP20: Ayle 3C 6
Coppice Way HP20: Ayle 3C 6
Coppidwell Dr. HP21: Ayle 2C 12
Corbetts Way OX9: Tha 4D 24
Corfe Cl. HP21: Ayle 2D 12
Cornbrook Rd. HP21: Ayle 2G 11
Corncrake HP19: Ayle 2A 6
Cornmarket OX9: Tha 3D 24
Coronation Vs. HP21: Ayle 5A 6
(off Highbridge Rd.)
Corrid Ind. Pk. HP19: Ayle 4F 5
Cosford M. HP22: Halt 3E 23
Cosy Corner HP22: Ast C 2D 14
Cotmore Cl. OX9: Tha 4F 25
Cotmore Fld. OX9: Tha 4F 25
Cotmore Gdns. OX9: Tha 4F 25
Cotswold Grn. HP20: Ayle 3A 6
(off Hilton Av.)
Cottage Grounds HP17: Sto 2C 10
Cottesloe Rd. HP21: Ayle 2H 11
Cottesloe Ter. HP21: Ayle 2A 12
(off Cottesloe Rd.)
Cottland Clay HP17: Hadd 2G 17
County Court
Aylesbury .4H 5
Court Cl. HP21: Ayle 6A 6
HP27: Prin R 2E 33
Courtmoor Cl. HP21: Ayle 1H 11
Courtyards, The HP22: Ast C 3E 15
Cousins Dr. HP20: Ayle 3B 6
Cousins Piece HP18: Che 1C 16
Coventon Rd. HP19: Ayle 3F 5
Cowleaze OX39: Chin 5B 30
Cowley Cl. HP22: Bier 2C 6
Coxhill Way HP21: Ayle 6H 5
Coy Ct. HP20: Ayle 5C 6
Cozens Cl. HP18: Long C 2A 16
Crabtree Rd. HP17: Hadd 4F 17
Cradle Footpath HP17: Elle, Gt Kim 2C 28
HP27: Whit, Gt Kim 5A 28
(not continuous)
Cradley Wlk. HP20: Ayle 2A 6
Crafton Pl. HP19: Ayle 4D 4
Craigwell Av. HP21: Ayle 6E 7

Cranley Cres. HP19: W'don 1G 5
Crendon Rd. HP18: Che 2C 16
Crendon Way HP18: Long C 5C 16
Crescent, The HP27: Prin R 2G 33
Creslow Way HP17: Sto 2A 10
Creswick Mdw. HP21: Ayle 2C 12
Crocus Dr. HP21: Ayle 2F 11
Croft, The HP17: Hadd 4F 17
Croft Cl. OX9: Tha 4E 25
Croft Ct. HP21: Ayle 6A 6
Croft Courtyard HP17: Hadd 4F 17
Croft Ho. HP21: Ayle 6A 6
Croft Pas. HP21: Ayle 6A 6
Croft Rd. HP21: Ayle 6A 6
   OX9: Tha 4E 25
Cromhamstone HP17: Sto 2B 10
Cromwell Av. HP19: Ayle 3G 5
   OX9: Tha 2E 25
Cromwell Ct. OX39: Chin 4D 30
   (off Lwr. Icknield Way)
Crosland Rd. HP21: Ayle 1D 12
Crossfield Rd. HP27: Prin R 1G 33
CROSS LANE 1G 31
Crowbrook Rd. HP27: Ask, Mon R 5F 27
CROWELL 6A 30
Crowell M. HP19: Ayle 5D 4
Crowell Rd. OX39: Chin 6B 30
Crown Court
   Aylesbury 5A 6
Crown Leys HP20: Ayle 4H 5
   (not continuous)
Cruickshank Dr. HP22: Halt 3D 22
Cubb Field HP19: Ayle 6F 5
Cubitt St. HP19: Ayle 4G 5
Cuckoo Way HP19: Ayle 5D 4
CUDDINGTON 4B 8
Cuddington Ct. HP18: Cudd 4B 8
Cuddington Hill HP18: Cudd 4A 8
Cuddington Rd. HP18: Dint 4E 9
Culpepper Cl. HP19: W'don 1G 5
Culverton Hill HP27: Prin R 2F 33
Culverton La. HP27: Prin R 4E 33
Cumberland Cl. HP21: Ayle 6D 6
Curlew HP19: Ayle 2B 6
Cursley Path HP19: Ayle 2B 6
Cuttle Brook Gdns. OX9: Tha 2C 24
Cuttle Brook Nature Reserve 3C 24
Cyclamen Pl. HP21: Ayle 2F 11

D

Dacre Rd. HP22: Halt 2E 23
Dadbrook HP18: Cudd 5B 8
Dadbrook Cl. HP18: Cudd 5B 8
Dadfield Cl. HP18: Cudd 5B 8
Dalesford Rd. HP21: Ayle 3C 12
Dalston Cl. HP20: Ayle 3B 6
Dalwood M. HP19: Ayle 5D 4
Daly Way HP20: Ayle 6D 6
Dancers End La. HP23: Tring 4H 15
Dancersend Nature Reserve 2G 23
Dane Ct. HP21: Ayle 3H 11
Dark La. HP18: Che 1C 16
Darley Cl. HP21: Ayle 1D 12
Dart Cl. HP21: Ayle 2G 11
David Cl. HP21: Ayle 3C 12
Davies Cl. HP20: Ayle 5H 5
Dawney Cl. HP19: Ayle 3G 5
Dean Cl. HP21: Ayle 2C 12
Dean Way HP22: Ast C 3F 15
Dearing Cl. HP20: Ayle 3B 6
Delamere Cl. HP20: Ayle 4H 5
Dell, The HP20: Ayle 3C 6
Denbigh Rd. OX9: Tha 2E 25
Denby Wlk. HP20: Ayle 5C 6
Dennis Cl. HP22: Ast C 3G 15
Derby Pl. HP18: Ayle 6B 4
Derwent Rd. HP21: Ayle 1D 12
Desborough Grn. HP20: Ayle 4H 5
   (off Lansdowne Rd.)
Devereux Pl. HP19: Ayle 3E 5
Deverill Rd. HP21: Ayle 4G 11
Devon Rd. HP19: Ayle 2E 5
Diane Cl. HP21: Ayle 3C 12
Diane Wlk. HP21: Ayle 3C 12
Dickens Way HP19: Ayle 3D 4
Dicks Way HP19: Ayle 2D 4
Digby Cl. OX9: Tha 2F 25
DINTON 5G 9
Discovery St. HP18: Ayle 6B 4
Disraeli Sq. HP19: Ayle 5E 5
Ditchingham Cl. HP19: Ayle 6F 5
Dixon Cl. HP21: Ayle 1F 11

Dobbins La. HP22: Wend 4A 22
Dollicott HP17: Hadd 3F 17
Dolphin Pl. HP21: Ayle 1A 12
Domino Way HP18: Ayle 6B 4
Dorchester Cl. HP22: Sto M 5D 12
Dorchester Pl. OX9: Tha 3D 24
Dormer Cl. HP21: Ayle 1F 11
Dormer Ct. HP20: Ayle 3B 6
Dormer Rd. OX9: Tha 5F 25
Dorrells Rd. HP27: Longw 5B 26
Dorset Pl. HP21: Ayle 1E 13
Douglas Rd. HP20: Ayle 3B 6
Dove Cl. HP21: Ayle 2G 11
Dovecote HP17: Hadd 3F 17
Dovecote Cl. HP17: Hadd 3F 17
   HP27: Mon R 6G 27
Dove Ho. HP19: Ayle 1B 6
   (off Dove Pl.)
Doveleat OX39: Chin 4D 30
Dove Pl. HP19: Ayle 1B 6
Dover Hedge HP21: Ayle 6E 7
Dragon Tail HP17: Hadd 4G 17
Drake Cl. HP21: Ayle 1F 11
Drakes Dr. HP18: Long C 5B 16
Drakes Farm HP18: Long C 4C 16
DRAYTON BEAUCHAMP 2H 15
Drayton Rd. HP20: Ayle 3H 5
Drewitt Pl. HP21: Ayle 2B 12
Druids Wlk. OX39: Chin 5C 30
Dryden Cl. HP21: Ayle 3A 6
Duck Farm Ct. HP20: Ayle 5H 5
Duck Sq. OX39: Chin 5C 30
Duke St. HP27: Prin R 1F 33
Dunbar Dr. OX9: Tha 2E 25
Dunsham La. HP19: Ayle 2B 6
   HP20: Ayle 3H 5
DUNSMORE 4H 29
Dunsmore Av. HP27: Mon R 6G 27
Dunsmore Ride HP27: Mon R 6F 27

E

Eagles Rd. HP20: Ayle 5C 6
Eames Cl. HP20: Ayle 2B 6
Earlswood Cl. HP21: Ayle 2C 12
Eascote Rd. HP21: Ayle 3D 12
Eastern St. HP20: Ayle 4A 6
Eastfield Rd. HP20: Ayle 5D 6
   HP27: Prin R 2G 33
East St. OX9: Tha 3E 25
Eaton Cl. HP22: West T 5H 13
Eaton Rd. HP21: Ayle 1H 11
Ebble Cl. HP21: Ayle 3G 11
Eden Cl. HP21: Ayle 3H 11
Edgecombe Rd. HP21: Ayle 2D 12
Edgehill OX9: Tha 1D 24
Edge St. HP19: Ayle 4G 5
Edinburgh Pl. HP21: Ayle 4C 4
Edison Rd. HP19: Ayle 4C 4
Edward Cl. HP21: Ayle 3C 12
Edward Wlk. HP21: Ayle 3C 12
Eeles Cl. HP21: Ayle 2D 4
Eggleton Cl. HP21: Ayle 2A 12
Egypt Way HP19: Ayle 5E 5
Elderdene OX39: Chin 3D 30
Eldridge La. HP17: But X 6E 21
Eleanor Gdns. HP21: Ayle 2A 18
Elham Way HP21: Ayle 3C 12
Eliot Cl. HP21: Ayle 3D 4
Elizabeth Cl. HP21: Ayle 3D 12
Ellen Pl. HP21: Ayle 2G 11
Ellen Rd. HP21: Ayle 1F 11
Ellen Wlk. HP21: Ayle 1F 11
   (off Thompson Cl.)
ELLESBOROUGH 1D 28
Ellesborough Golf Course 6F 21
Ellesborough Rd. HP17: But X, Elle, Lit K ..2B 28
   HP22: Wend 6H 21
Elm Brook Cl. HP18: Che 2D 16
Elm Cl. HP17: But X 6E 21
   HP22: West T 5H 13
   OX39: Chin 6C 30
Elm Ct. HP17: But X 5H 13
Elmdale Gdns. HP27: Prin R 2F 33
Elm Dr. OX39: Chin 6C 30
Elm Farm Rd. HP21: Ayle 2B 12
Elm Grn. HP21: Ayle 1H 11
ELMHURST 3A 6
Elmhurst Rd. HP20: Ayle 3H 5
Elm Rd. HP27: Prin R 2F 33
Elms, The HP20: Ayle 3A 6
Elms Rd. OX9: Tha 3D 24
Elm Trees HP18: Long C 2A 16

Elsmore Cl. HP21: Ayle 3D 12
Ely Rd. HP22: Halt 3E 23
Ember Path HP21: Ayle 3G 11
Emmett Dr. HP21: Ayle 2A 12
EMMINGTON 1A 30
Emmington OX39: Chin 2A 30
Enborne Cl. HP21: Ayle 3H 11
Ensbury Path HP20: Ayle 3A 6
Eskdale Rd. HP22: Sto M 5D 12
Essex Ho. HP20: Ayle 4H 5
Essex Pl. HP19: Ayle 2E 5
Essex Rd. OX9: Tha 4F 25
Estover Way OX39: Chin 5B 30
Evans Cl. HP18: Che 1C 16
   HP21: Ayle 3C 12
Evenlode Cl. HP21: Ayle 2G 11
Evesham Grn. HP19: Ayle 2G 5
Evett Cl. HP21: Ayle 4B 6
Exchange St. HP20: Ayle 5A 6
Eyre Cl. HP19: Ayle 5D 4
Eythrope Pk. 4A 4
Eythrope Rd. HP17: Sto 1A 10

F

Fairfax Cl. OX9: Tha 3E 25
Fairfax Cres. HP20: Ayle 3A 6
FAIRFORD LEYS 5D 4
Fairford Leys Way HP19: Ayle 6E 5
Fairmile HP21: Ayle 6C 6
Fairway HP27: Prin R 2E 33
Faithfull Cl. HP17: Sto 2A 10
Falcon, The HP19: Ayle 1B 6
Fall Cl. HP19: Ayle 2H 5
Fanshawe Rd. OX9: Tha 3F 25
Faraday Rd. HP19: Ayle 3D 4
Far Furlong Cl. HP21: Ayle 4H 11
Farmbrough Cl. HP21: Ayle 4C 6
Farm Pl. OX39: Hent 2E 31
Farnley Rd. HP20: Ayle 3A 6
Fells Cl. HP18: Long C 3B 16
Fern La. HP17: Hadd 3G 17
Field Cl. HP20: Ayle 3C 6
Field End HP18: Long C 4C 16
Fieldfare HP19: Ayle 1A 6
Field Way HP20: Ayle 3C 6
Fiesta End HP18: Ayle 6B 4
Finmere Cres. HP21: Ayle 2E 13
Firecrest Way HP19: Ayle 4D 4
Firs, The HP22: Bier 1E 7
Firs Ct. HP22: Bier 1E 7
Fish Ponds La. OX9: Tha 2C 24
Flaxen Fld. HP22: West T 5H 13
FLEET MARSTON 1A 4
Fleet St. HP20: Ayle 4H 5
Fleetwood Way OX9: Tha 1D 24
Fleming Rd. HP22: Halt 3D 22
Fletcher Cl. HP19: Ayle 2D 4
Flint Hollow OX39: Chin 5B 30
Flint St. HP17: Hadd 4F 17
Florence Ct. HP19: Ayle 4H 5
   (off Willow Rd.)
FLORENCE NIGHTINGALE HOUSE (HOSPICE)
   ....3B 12
   (WITHIN STOKE MANDEVILLE HOSPITAL)
Florey Gdns. HP20: Ayle 5B 6
FORD 2A 18
FORD, THE 1A 32
Ford Rd. HP17: Dint 4H 9
   HP17: Ford, Sto 6A 10
Forest Cl. HP22: Wend 5B 22
   HP27: Prin R 2G 33
   (off Chestnut Rd.)
Foresters OX39: Chin 5B 30
FORT END 2F 17
Forty Grn. HP27: Bled 1G 31
Foskett Way HP21: Ayle 2A 12
Foster Cl. HP20: Ayle 3B 6
Fothergill Pl. OX9: Tha 3D 24
Founders Path HP19: Ayle 2G 5
Fountain Ct. HP20: Ayle 5H 5
   (off Buckingham St.)
Fowler Rd. HP19: Ayle 5F 5
Fox Cover OX39: Chin 5C 30
Foxgloves HP21: Ayle 2F 11
Franklin Cl. HP17: Hadd 2G 17
Franklin Rd. HP17: Hadd 2G 17
Fraucup Cl. HP17: Ford 2A 18
Fremantle Rd. HP21: Ayle 2A 12
Friarage Pas. HP20: Ayle 5H 5
   (off Bourbon St.)
Friarage Rd. HP20: Ayle 5H 5
Friarscroft Way HP20: Ayle 5G 5

Friars Furlong HP18: Long C 2A **16**
Friars Sq. HP20: Ayle 5H **5**
Friday Ct. OX9: Tha 2D **24**
Frobisher Ct. *HP19: Ayle* *4H 5*
(off Buckingham Rd.)
Frog La. HP18: Cudd 4B **8**
Frogmore La. HP18: Long C 4A **16**
Frome Cl. HP21: Ayle 2G **11**
Fuggle Dr. HP21: Ayle 2A **12**
Fulmar Pl. *HP19: Ayle* *2B 6*
(off Watermeadow)
Furlong Cres. HP17: Bish 6E **11**
Furlongs, The OX9: More 5A **24**
Furrow Cl. HP21: Ayle 3H **11**

G

Gables, The HP17: Hadd 4G **17**
Gables Cl. HP22: Wend 5A **22**
Gadge Cl. OX9: Tha 2C **24**
Gainsborough Pl. HP19: Ayle 2D **4**
Gainsborough Rd. HP21: Ayle 3A **12**
Gala Bingo
Aylesbury 5A **6**
Galloway HP19: Ayle 2E **5**
Galsworthy Pl. HP19: Ayle 3D **4**
Garden City OX9: Tha 4F **25**
Garden Cl. HP22: Halt 1C **22**
Gardner Cl. HP19: Ayle 2E **5**
Garland Way HP22: Ast C 2E **15**
Garron Cl. HP21: Ayle 4H **11**
Garside Way HP20: Ayle 4C **6**
Gas All. OX9: Tha 3E **25**
Gatehouse Cl. HP19: Ayle 5G **5**
Gatehouse Ind. Area
HP19: Ayle 4F **5**
Gatehouse Rd. HP19: Ayle 4G **5**
Gatehouse Way HP19: Ayle 4F **5**
Gatensbury Pl. HP27: Prin R 2F **33**
Gates Orchard HP22: Ast C 2D **14**
Gateway, The HP19: Ayle 4F **5**
George St. HP20: Ayle 5H **5**
Gib La. HP22: Bier 1F **7**
GIBRALTAR .4F **9**
Gibson La. HP17: Hadd 4G **17**
Gibson Row HP19: Ayle 5D **4**
Giffard Way HP18: Long C 2A **16**
Giles Rd. HP22: Halt 3D **22**
Gilliflower St. HP21: Ayle 6B **4**
Gillions Pl. HP21: Ayle 6D **6**
Gilmore Rd. HP20: Ayle 2A **6**
Gingers Cl. HP22: Ast C 2E **15**
Glaven Rd. HP21: Ayle 3G **11**
Glebe, The HP17: Sto 2A **10**
HP22: West T 5H **13**
Glenfield Cl. HP21: Ayle 2C **12**
Glenham Rd. OX9: Tha 3F **25**
Glimbers Gro. OX39: Chin 5C **30**
Glynswood OX39: Chin 5C **30**
Goffe Cl. OX9: Tha 3F **25**
Gogh Rd. HP19: Ayle 3C **4**
Goldcrest HP19: Ayle 1B **6**
Golden Hills OX39: Chin 5D **30**
Goldsmith Cl. HP21: Ayle 2A **12**
Golf Club La. HP27: Whit 6A **28**
Goodson Ind. M. OX9: Tha 3D **4**
Goodwin Rd. HP19: Ayle 5G **5**
Goosen Grn. HP21: Ayle 1E **13**
Gowers Fld. HP20: Ayle 4H **5**
Goya Pl. HP19: Ayle 3D **4**
Grafton Orchard OX39: Chin 4D **30**
Grafton Rd. HP19: Ayle 3E **5**
Granary Yd. HP18: Long C 3A **16**
Grange Gdns. HP22: Wend 4B **22**
Grangelands & Pulpit Hill Nature Reserve
. . . . .4B **28**
Grange Sports Centre, The 6B **6**
Grange Vw. HP27: Ask 4A **28**
Granville Pl. HP20: Ayle 5H **5**
Granville St. HP20: Ayle 5H **5**
Grasmere HP21: Ayle 2D **12**
Grass Hays HP21: Ayle 6E **7**
Grasslands HP20: Ayle 4C **6**
Gravel Dr. HP23: Tring 4H **15**
Great Ground HP18: Ayle 1B **4**
GREAT KIMBLE 2A **28**
Great La. HP22: Bier 1C **6**
HP22: Wend 5B **22**
Gt. Meadow Way HP19: Ayle 5D **4**
Great Stone HP18: Cudd 4B **8**
Gt. Western St. HP20: Ayle 5H **5**
Grebe Cl. HP19: Ayle 2B **6**
Grecian St. HP20: Ayle 5C **6**

Green, The HP17: Dint 6G **9**
HP18: Che 1C **16**
HP18: Cudd 4B **8**
HP27: Longw 5B **26**
Green Acre HP21: Ayle 6C **6**
Green End HP20: Ayle 5H **5**
Green End St. HP22: Ast C 2D **14**
Green La. HP17: Hadd 6E **9**
HP27: Longw 2A **26**
Green Pk. 4E **15**
Green Pk. HP22: Ast C 4E **15**
Greens Keep HP17: Hadd 3F **17**
Greensleeves Dr. HP18: Ayle 6B **4**
Green Vw. HP20: Ayle 3C **6**
Greenway HP17: Hadd 4F **17**
OX9: Tha 2D **24**
Greenwood, The HP22: Ast C 2D **14**
Greenwood Av. OX39: Chin 6C **30**
Greenwood Mdw. OX39: Chin 5D **30**
Greetham Rd. HP21: Ayle 1E **13**
Grenadier Path HP18: Ayle 6B **4**
Grendon Way HP22: Bier 1C **6**
Grenville Av. HP22: Wend 2A **22**
Grenville Grn. HP21: Ayle 3H **11**
Grenville Rd. HP21: Ayle 2G **11**
Grenville Way OX9: Tha 2F **25**
Greyhound La. OX9: Tha 2D **24**
Greyhound Wlk. OX9: Tha 2D **24**
Griffin Ind. Mall HP19: Ayle 4F **5**
Griffin La. HP19: Ayle 5E **5**
Griffin La. Ind. Est. HP19: Ayle 4F **5**
Griffin Pl. HP19: Ayle 4F **5**
Griffin Rd. OX9: Tha 3G **25**
Griffiths Acre HP17: Sto 2C **10**
Grimmer Cl. HP19: Ayle 2D **4**
Grosvenor Way HP19: Ayle 4C **4**
Grove Ct. HP22: Bier 1E **7**
Grove La. HP17: Gt Kim, Lit K 2H **27**
Grovers Ct. HP27: Prin R 3E **33**
Groves Cl. HP22: Halt 2E **23**
Guernsey Cl. HP19: Ayle 2E **5**
Guillemot Cl. HP19: Ayle 2A **6**
Guillemot Way HP19: Ayle 2A **6**
Gull Way HP19: Ayle 2B **6**
Gurney Cl. HP20: Ayle 3B **6**
Guttmann Rd. HP21: Ayle 2B **12**
Gwendolyn Buck Dr. HP21: Ayle 3B **12**

H

HADDENHAM 3F **17**
Haddenham and Thame Parkway Station (Rail)
. . . . .3E **17**
Haddenham Bus. Pk.
HP17: Hadd 2F **17**
Haddington Cl. HP22: Halt 4D **22**
Haddington Way HP20: Ayle 4C **6**
Haggar St. HP17: Sto 2A **10**
Haglis Dr. HP22: Wend 3A **22**
Hailey Cft. OX39: Chin 5B **30**
Haines Cl. HP19: Ayle 3D **4**
Hale La. HP22: Wend 6D **22**
HP23: St Leo 6D **22**
Hale Leys HP20: Ayle 5A **6**
Hale Rd. HP22: Wend 5C **22**
Hales Cft. HP21: Ayle 3D **12**
Halt St. HP20: Ayle 5A **6**
HALTON 1C **22**
HALTON CAMP 2E **23**
Halton La.
HP22: Wend, Halt 2A **22**
HP22: West T 4A **14**
Halton Stadium (Sports Arena) 1B **22**
Halton Tennis Cen. 6C **14**
Halton Wood Rd. HP22: Halt 4E **23**
Hambledon Cl. HP21: Ayle 2D **12**
Hamble Dr. HP21: Ayle 2G **11**
Hamilton Ct. HP19: Ayle 3H **5**
Hamilton Ho. *HP19: Ayle* *4E 5*
(off Broadfields)
Hamilton Rd. OX9: Tha 2E **25**
Hampden Av. OX9: Tha 4D **24**
Hampden Cl. HP21: Ayle 1H **11**
HP22: Sto M 6D **12**
Hampden Gdns. HP21: Ayle 1H **11**
Hampden Rd. HP21: Ayle 1H **11**
HP22: Sto M 5D **12**
HP22: Wend 5C **22**
Hampden Sq. HP19: Ayle 5E **5**
Hampstead Cl. HP19: Ayle 4D **4**
Hancock Cl. HP21: Ayle 2A **12**
Hannon Rd. HP21: Ayle 2G **11**
Hanover Cl. HP19: Ayle 3E **5**

Hanover Ct. *HP21: Ayle* *5A 6*
(off Croft Pas.)
Hanson Way HP21: Ayle 3C **12**
Harbourne Cl. HP21: Ayle 4G **11**
Harcourt Grn. HP19: Ayle 3F **5**
Hardy Cl. HP21: Ayle 6A **6**
Harebridge La. HP22: Halt 5E **15**
Harrier Cl. HP19: Ayle 2B **6**
Harris Ct. HP20: Ayle 3B **6**
Harrison Pl. OX9: Tha 2D **24**
Harroell HP18: Long C 4B **16**
(Abbot Wlk.)
HP18: Long C 3B **16**
(Fells Cl.)
Harrow Cl. HP21: Ayle 3A **12**
Harts Rd. HP17: Hadd 3H **17**
HARTWELL .2D **10**
Hartwell End HP21: Ayle 6F **5**
(not continuous)
Harvey Rd. HP21: Ayle 2A **12**
Haslerig Cl. HP21: Ayle 2B **12**
Hastoe Pk. HP20: Ayle 3B **6**
Havelock St. HP20: Ayle 4H **5**
Haven Shaw Cl. HP21: Ayle 2C **12**
Hawfinch HP19: Ayle 2A **6**
Hawkslade Furlong HP21: Ayle 4H **11**
Hawthorn Av. OX9: Tha 3C **24**
Hawthorn Cl. HP20: Ayle 4B **6**
Hawthorn Rd. HP27: Prin R 2G **33**
Hawthorns, The HP27: Mon R 4G **27**
HAYDON HILL 3C **4**
Haydon Rd. HP19: Ayle 3G **5**
Hayter Cl. HP19: W'don 1G **5**
Haywood Way HP19: Ayle 2D **4**
Hazel Av. OX9: Tha 3C **24**
Hazeldene HP22: Wend 5C **22**
Hazell Av. HP21: Ayle 6C **6**
Hazelrig Dr. OX9: Tha 3E **25**
Hazelton Cl. OX9: Tha 3C **24**
Hazlehurst Dr. HP21: Ayle 2C **12**
Heath Cl. HP21: Ayle 2D **12**
Heather Wlk. *HP21: Ayle* *1F 11*
(off Primrose Dr.)
Hedge Furlong HP17: Hadd 3G **17**
Hedgerley OX39: Chin 5B **30**
Hedley Cl. HP22: Ast C 3G **15**
Helford Cl. HP22: Wend 3H **11**
Hemingway Rd. HP19: Ayle 3D **4**
Hemlock Cl. HP22: Sto M 3E **13**
Hemp Hill HP19: Ayle 5E **5**
HEMTON WAINHILL 4G **31**
Henrietta Rd. OX9: Tha 2E **25**
Henry Rd. HP20: Ayle 5D **6**
HENTON 1E **31**
Henton M. HP19: Ayle 5E **5**
Hereford Way HP19: Ayle 2E **5**
Hernes Oak OX39: Chin 3D **30**
Heron, The HP19: Ayle 1A **6**
Heron Cl. HP20: Ayle 5E **7**
Heron Path HP22: Wend 5B **22**
Herston Cl. HP21: Ayle 2D **12**
Hickman St. HP19: Ayle 5D **4**
Highbridge Rd. HP21: Ayle 5A **6**
Highbridge Wlk. HP21: Ayle 5A **6**
Highfield HP18: Long C 3A **16**
Highfield Cl. OX9: Tha 3A **24**
Highfield Rd. HP27: Prin R 1G **33**
Highgate M. HP19: Ayle 4D **4**
High Moors HP22: Halt 1B **22**
High St. HP17: Dint 5G **9**
HP17: Hadd 4F **17**
HP18: Long C 3A **16**
HP20: Ayle 5H **5**
HP22: Wend 5B **22**
HP27: Prin R 2F **33**
OX9: Tha 2C **24**
OX39: Chin 4D **30**
Hikers Way HP18: Long C 5D **16**
Hilda Wharf HP20: Ayle 5A **6**
Hillary Cl. HP21: Ayle 2C **12**
Hill Farm Ct. OX39: Chin 5D **30**
Hillier Rd. HP21: Ayle 4H **11**
Hillington Cl. HP19: Ayle 6F **5**
Hill Rd. OX39: Chin 5D **30**
Hillside Cotts. HP18: Cudd 5B **8**
Hillside Vw. OX39: Chin 6D **30**
Hilltop HP18: Long C 4B **16**
Hill Top La. OX39: Chin 6F **31**
Hill Vw. HP17: Gt Kim 2H **27**
Hillwerke OX39: Chin 5C **30**
Hilton Av. HP20: Ayle 3A **6**
Hinds Way HP21: Ayle 1F **11**
HMYOI Aylesbury HP20: Ayle 4B **6**
Hogtrough La. HP22: Wend 6C **22**

Holland Cl. HP22: Wend 5B 22
  OX39: Chin 3D 30
Holland Rd. HP19: Ayle 3F 5
Holliers Cl. OX9: Tha 3D 24
  OX9: Tow 4H 25
Hollington HP18: Long C 3A 16
Hollins Ct. HP19: Ayle 4G 5
Holloway, The HP27: Whit 5H 27
Holly Blue M. HP19: W'don 1F 5
Holly Ct. HP22: Wend 4C 22
Holly Dr. HP21: Ayle 1A 12
Holly Grn. La. HP27: Bled 1G 31
Holly Tree La. HP18: Cudd 4B 8
Holman St. HP19: Ayle 2G 5
Home Cl. HP22: West T 5H 13
Home Fld. HP19: Ayle 6E 5
Homestead, The OX9: Tha 2C 24
Homestead Cl. HP17: Upt 3H 9
Homestead Pl. HP19: Ayle 5E 5
Honey Banks HP22: Wend 5C 22
Honour Cl. HP20: Ayle 3B 6
Hoods Farm Cl. HP22: Bier 1E 7
Hope Pl. HP22: Halt 3E 23
Hopkins Ct. HP20: Ayle 3B 6
Hopton Rd. OX9: Tha 2E 25
Hordern Cl. HP17: Hadd 3F 17
Hornbeam Way HP22: Sto M 3E 13
Horns La. HP27: Prin R 2F 33
HORSENDEN 2C 32
Horsenden La. HP27: Prin R 3C 32
Horseshoes Pl. OX9: Tha 4E 25
Horton Av. OX9: Tha 4E 25
Horton Cl. HP19: Ayle 6E 5
  OX9: Tha 4E 25
Howard Av. HP21: Ayle 1D 12
Howards Hill Grn. HP19: W'don 1H 5
  (off Colonial Grantham Av.)
Howland Rd. OX9: Tha 5F 25
Howletts Cl. HP19: Ayle 6E 5
Hudson M. HP19: Ayle 4C 4
Hughenden Grn. HP21: Ayle 3A 12
Hulbert End HP21: Ayle 2F 13
Hulcombe Wlk. HP20: Ayle 3A 6
Hulcott La. HP22: Bier 1F 7
Hull Cl. HP21: Ayle 1A 12
Humber Dr. HP21: Ayle 2G 11
Hunters Point OX39: Chin 5C 30
Hunt Rd. OX9: Tha 4F 25
Hyde, The HP22: West T 5H 13
Hyton Sq. HP19: W'don 1H 5
  (off Acres Way)

I

Icknield Cl. HP22: Wend 4C 22
Icknield Ct. HP27: Prin R 1G 33
Icknield Way OX39: Chin 5E 31
Ingram Av. HP21: Ayle 1E 13
Innkeepers Ct. HP27: Longw 4B 26
Intalbury Av. HP19: Ayle 3E 5
Ireton Ct. OX9: Tha 2D 24
Iris Cl. HP21: Ayle 2F 11
Iris Ct. HP20: Ayle 5D 6
Irvine Dr. HP22: Sto M 5C 12
Irving Path HP19: Ayle 4G 5
Isis Cl. HP21: Ayle 4H 11
Ivinghoe Vw. HP20: Ayle 4B 6
Ivy Cl. HP27: Longw 6C 26
Ivy La. HP22: Bro 4F 7

J

Jackson Pl. HP22: Halt 3D 22
Jackson Rd. HP19: Ayle 2D 4
Jakeman Way HP21: Ayle 1F 11
Jane Cl. HP21: Ayle 3C 12
Jane Morbey Rd. OX9: Tha 4E 25
Jannetta Cl. HP21: Ayle 6D 6
Jansel Sq. HP21: Ayle 1D 12
Jardines Ten Pin Bowling Club 5H 5
  (off Silver St.)
Jarvis Cl. HP21: Ayle 1C 12
Jasmine Cl. HP21: Ayle 3C 12
Jasmine Cres. HP27: Prin R 2F 33
Jeannie Arm Rd. HP22: Halt 3D 22
Jefferies Rd. HP17: Sto 2A 10
Jefferson Way OX9: Tha 4E 25
Jeffrey Wlk. HP19: Ayle 6E 5
Jenner Rd. HP21: Ayle 2A 12
Jesse's La. HP18: Long C 3B 16
John Fitzjohn Av. HP18: Ayle 1B 4
Jordans M. HP19: Ayle 4G 5

Jubilee Gdns. OX9: Tha 3B 24
Juniper Dr. HP22: Sto M 3E 13
Juson's Glebe HP22: Wend 4C 22

K

Kanton Ct. HP19: Ayle 3G 5
Keats Cl. HP21: Ayle 1B 12
Keble Cl. HP19: Ayle 5F 5
Keen Cl. HP19: Ayle 5E 5
Keens La. OX39: Chin 5D 30
Kempson Cl. HP19: Ayle 4F 5
Kemps Piece HP17: Hadd 3G 17
Kendal Cl. HP21: Ayle 1D 12
Kenilworth Dr. HP19: Ayle 3H 5
Kennet Cl. HP21: Ayle 3G 11
Kensington Path HP19: Ayle 4D 4
  (off Spruce Cl.)
Kentmere Rd. HP21: Ayle 6D 6
Kerr Pl. HP21: Ayle 6A 6
Kerry Cl. HP19: Ayle 2E 5
Kestrel Way HP19: Ayle 1A 6
Ketchmere Cl. HP18: Long C 3A 16
Kiln Av. OX39: Chin 6D 30
  (not continuous)
Kilner Rd. HP21: Ayle 2A 12
Kimble Pk. HP17: Lit K 6A 20
Kimble Pk. Rd. HP17: Lit K 6A 20
KIMBLE WICK 5E 19
Kimblewick Rd.
  HP17: Gt Kim, Kim W 5E 19
King Edward Av. HP21: Ayle 6C 6
Kingfisher HP21: Ayle 1A 6
Kingsash Rd. HP19: Ayle 5D 4
Kingsbury HP20: Ayle 5H 5
King's Cl. OX9: Tha 3D 24
KINGSEY .6G 17
Kingsey Rd. OX9: Tha, Tow 3E 25
Kingsgate HP19: Ayle 5E 5
King's Head Inn 5H 5
  (off Market Sq.)
King's Head Pas. HP20: Ayle 5H 5
  (off Temple St.)
Kingsland Rd. HP21: Ayle 3C 12
Kingsmead HP27: Mon R 5F 27
Kings Mdw. HP22: Bier 1E 7
Kings Oak Cl. HP27: Mon R 5G 27
King's Rd. HP21: Ayle 5B 6
  OX9: Tha 3E 25
Kinson Grn. HP20: Ayle 2A 6
Kittiwake HP19: Ayle 1A 6
Knightsbridge Pl. HP19: Ayle 5E 5
Kop Hill HP27: Prin R 2H 33
Kyle End HP21: Ayle 2A 12
Kynaston Av. HP21: Ayle 4A 12

L

Lacemakers HP18: Long C 3A 16
  OX39: Chin 5C 30
Lacemakers Ct. HP27: Prin R 2F 33
Lacey Dr. OX9: Tha 4F 25
Ladbroke Cl. HP20: Ayle 3A 6
Lakeside HP19: Ayle 1A 6
Lakeside Rd. OX39: Chin 6D 30
Lambe Rd. HP22: Halt 3E 23
Lambert Wlk. OX9: Tha 2D 24
Lambourne Av. HP21: Ayle 4H 11
Lammas La. HP18: Che 1C 16
Lammas Path HP18: Che 1C 16
Lancaster Rd. HP21: Ayle 1D 12
Lander Rd. HP19: Ayle 2D 4
Lane, The OX39: Chin 4D 30
Langdale Rd. OX9: Tha 3E 25
Langdon Av. HP21: Ayle 2D 12
Langstone Cl. HP20: Ayle 2B 6
Langstone Cl. HP20: Ayle 2B 6
Lansdowne Rd. HP20: Ayle 3H 5
Larch Cl. HP20: Ayle 3C 6
Lark Va. HP19: Ayle 2A 6
Lashlake Rd. OX9: Tha 2D 24
Laurel Way HP21: Ayle 6A 6
Lautrec Way HP19: Ayle 3D 4
Lavender Cl. HP21: Ayle 2F 11
Lavender Wlk. HP21: Ayle 1F 11
  (off Lavender Cl.)
Lavric Rd. HP21: Ayle 1G 11
Lawrence Rd. HP20: Ayle 3B 6
Lay Rd. HP19: Ayle 2F 5
Leach Rd. HP21: Ayle 6G 5
Lea La. HP18: Long C 5C 16
Lee Ct. OX9: Tha 3D 24

Lee Cres. HP17: Sto 2B 10
Lee Rd. HP21: Ayle 1H 11
  HP27: Saun 6C 32
Leith Rd. HP19: Ayle 5E 5
Lembrook Wlk. HP21: Ayle 1G 11
Leonard Pulham Ho.
  HP22: Halt 2D 22
Leonard W. Path HP21: Ayle 6B 6
Letter Box La. HP27: Ask 4H 27
Leverkus Ct. OX39: Chin 5D 30
Levings Cl. HP19: Ayle 2E 5
Lewis Cl. HP19: W'don 1H 5
Leyburne Gdns. OX39: Chin 4C 30
Leyfield Rd. HP21: Ayle 1A 12
Leys, The HP22: Halt 6C 14
Leys Cl. HP19: W'don 1G 5
Liffre Dr. HP22: Wend 3B 22
Ligo Av. HP22: Sto M 5E 13
Lime Gro. OX39: Chin 5D 30
Limelight Av. HP18: Ayle 5B 4
Limelight Theatre 5B 6
  (in Queens Pk. Arts Cen.)
Lime Rd. HP27: Prin R 2F 33
Limes, The HP22: Sto M 5D 12
Limes Av. HP21: Ayle 6D 6
Limmings La. OX9: Tha 4E 25
Lincoln Cl. HP22: Sto M 5D 12
Lincoln Pl. OX9: Tha 3D 24
Linden End HP21: Ayle 1B 12
Linden Lea HP22: Wend 3B 22
Lionel Av. HP22: Wend 4A 22
Lionel Cl. HP22: Wend 4A 22
Lisburn Path HP20: Ayle 3B 6
Lister Grn. HP21: Ayle 2A 12
  (off Jenner Rd.)
Little Cl. HP19: Ayle 4H 5
Little Gibbs HP27: Bled 1G 31
Little Ground HP18: Ayle 1B 4
Little Ham La. HP27: Mon R 6F 27
Lit. Hampden Cl. HP22: Wend 5B 22
LITTLE KIMBLE 6A 20
Little Kimble Station (Rail) 1A 28
Lit. Orchard Cl. HP27: Longw 6C 26
Little Orchards HP20: Ayle 2B 6
Little Park HP27: Prin R 2G 33
Locke Cl. HP19: Ayle 3E 5
Lodden Cl. HP21: Ayle 4H 11
Lodge Farm Cl. HP22: West T 5G 13
Lodge Hill .3F 29
Lodge Path HP19: Ayle 5D 4
London Cl. HP21: Ayle 6B 6
London Rd. HP22: Ast C 2D 14
  HP22: Wend 6C 22
LONG CRENDON 3B 16
Long Crendon Court House 2B 16
Long Crendon Ind. Est.
  HP18: Long C 4C 16
Long Crendon Rd. HP18: Long C 5B 16
  (Drakes Dr.)
  HP18: Long C 4A 16
  (Frogmore La.)
  OX9: Tha .5B 16
Longcroft HP22: Ast C 2E 15
Longcroft Av. HP22: Halt 3D 22
Longdown Hill HP27: Whit 5B 28
Longdown M. HP19: Ayle 5D 4
Long Furlong HP17: Hadd 3F 17
  HP17: Sto 2A 10
Long Hide HP27: Prin R 1G 33
Long Leys HP19: Ayle 5E 5
Long Lional HP20: Ayle 5A 6
Long Meadow HP21: Ayle 1D 12
Long Mdw. Cl. HP27: Mon R 5G 27
Long Plough HP22: Ast C 2D 14
Long Wall HP17: Hadd 4F 17
LONGWICK 5B 26
Longwick Rd. HP27: Longw, Prin R 5D 26
Loosley Grn. HP21: Ayle 3B 12
LOOSLEY ROW 6H 33
Lott Meadow HP21: Ayle 4H 11
Lott Walk HP21: Ayle 4H 11
  (off Lott Meadow)
Lovers Wlk. HP20: Ayle 5A 6
Lowbrook Cl. HP21: Ayle 3C 12
Lowe Gdns. HP21: Ayle 1H 11
LOWER CADSDEN 5B 28
Lwr. Church St. HP18: Cudd 4B 8
Lower Cl. HP19: Ayle 6F 5
LOWER END 2A 16
Lwr. Farm Ga. HP17: Upt 4H 9
Lower Grn. HP18: Cudd 4B 8
  HP22: West T 4A 14
Lower Grn. La. HP18: Che 1C 16
LOWER HARTWELL 1C 10

Lwr. Icknield Way HP17: Gt Kim 5D 26
  HP22: Ast C, B'land, Wils 3F 15
  HP23: Wils 1G 15
  HP27: Bled, Longw, Owls 1H 31
  OX39: Chin, Hent 4D 30
  OX39: Crow 6A 30
Lower Rd. HP17: Ford, B'land . . . . . .3H 17 & 6H 9
  HP21: Ayle 3A 12
  HP22: Sto M 3A 12
  HP27: Loos 6H 33
  OX39: Chin 4C 30
LOWER WAINHILL 4F 31
LOWER WINCHENDON 2A 8
Low La. HP17: Cudd 4C 8
  HP18: Cudd 4C 8
Lowmon Way HP21: Ayle 3H 11
Lowndes Path HP19: Ayle 5D 4
  (off Gt. Meadow Way)
Lucky La. HP20: Ayle 4H 5
Ludlow Dr. OX9: Tha 2E 25
Ludlow Pl. HP20: Ayle 5E 7
Ludsden Gro. OX9: Tha 3E 25
Lupin Cl. HP21: Ayle 1F 11
  (off Primrose Dr.)
Lupin Wlk. HP21: Ayle 2F 11
Lupton Rd. OX9: Tha 5E 25
Lyde End HP27: Bled 2H 31
Lydiard Cl. HP21: Ayle 3D 12
Lynher Cl. HP21: Ayle 3G 11
Lynwood Rd. HP21: Ayle 2C 12

M

McEwen Ride HP22: Halt 1C 22
McIndoe Dr. HP22: Halt 3D 22
Madeley Rd. HP21: Ayle 1A 12
Magistrates' Court
  Aylesbury 6A 6
Main Rd. HP17: Ford 2A 18
  HP22: B'land 1E 15
Main St. HP22: West T 5G 13
Maitland Rd. HP22: Halt 2D 22
Malford Cres. HP19: Ayle 1G 5
Mallard Cl. HP19: Ayle 1A 6
Mallard Cft. HP17: Hadd 2G 17
Malthouse Sq. HP27: Prin R 1F 33
Malvern Rd. HP20: Ayle 5E 7
Malyns Cl. OX39: Chin 4C 30
Mandeville M. HP21: Ayle 3A 12
Mandeville Rd. HP21: Ayle 1A 12
Mandeville School Sports Centre, The . .3H 11
Manor, The HP18: Long C 4A 16
Manor Cl. HP27: Bled 2H 31
Manor Cres. HP22: Wend 4C 22
Manor Dr. HP20: Ayle 3B 6
Mnr. Farm Cl. HP17: Sto 2B 10
  HP22: West T 5G 13
Manor House 1F 33
MANOR HOUSE 4B 6
Manor Ho. Cl. HP20: Ayle 4B 6
MANOR PARK 4A 6
Manor Pk. Av. HP27: Prin R 3E 33
Manor Rd. HP20: Ayle 4A 6
  HP22: Wend 4C 22
  HP27: Prin R 3E 33
Manor Vs. HP18: Che 1C 16
Mansion Hill HP22: Halt 1E 23
Maple End HP22: Sto M 3E 13
Maple Rd. OX9: Tha 3B 24
Maples, The HP22: Wend 4C 22
  (off Clay La.)
March Pl. HP19: Ayle 5F 5
Margaret Lowe Pl. HP22: Ast C 2E 15
Market Sq. HP20: Ayle 5H 5
  HP27: Prin R 2F 33
Market St. HP20: Ayle 5H 5
Markham Cl. HP19: Ayle 6E 5
Marlborough Rd. HP21: Ayle 3A 12
Marriott's Cl. HP17: Hadd 3F 17
Marriott's La. HP17: Hadd 3F 17
Marriott's Way HP17: Hadd 3F 17
Marroway HP22: West T 6F 13
MARSH 2H 19
Marshalls Lea HP22: Bier 2E 7
Marsham Cl. HP21: Ayle 3C 12
Marsh La. HP17: Bish 1H 19
  HP22: Sto M 1A 20
Marshment Cl. HP22: Ast C 2D 14
Marsh Rd. HP17: Lit K, Mars 3H 19
Marston Rd. OX9: Tha 2E 25
Mason's Ct. HP19: Ayle 6F 5
Masters Cl. OX9: Tha 2C 24
Masters Ho. HP21: Ayle 6H 5

Matlock Rd. HP20: Ayle 3B 6
Matthews Cl. HP20: Ayle 3B 6
Mayflower Cl. HP17: Hart 2D 10
Mead Acre HP27: Mon R 6F 27
Mead Cl. HP27: Mon R 5F 27
MEADLE 3F 27
Meadoway HP17: Hart 2D 10
Meadowbank Cl. HP18: Long C 2A 16
Meadow Cl. HP20: Ayle 4C 6
Meadowcroft HP19: Ayle 3E 5
  OX9: Tha 3F 25
Meadow Dr. HP27: Longw 5B 26
Meadow La. HP18: Long C 5C 16
Meadow Pk. HP22: Sto M 5E 13
Meadow Rd. OX39: Chin 5D 30
Meadow Vw. HP18: Long C 5C 16
Meadow Way HP20: Ayle 4C 6
  OX9: Tha 2D 24
Megdale Pl. HP20: Ayle 3H 5
Melbourne Cl. HP21: Ayle 2A 12
Melford Grn. HP19: Ayle 2G 5
Mellstock Rd. HP21: Ayle 2B 12
Melrose Wlk. HP21: Ayle 2B 12
Mentmore Grn. HP21: Ayle 4A 12
Mercers Mdw. HP22: Wend 3B 22
Meredith Dr. HP19: Ayle 3D 4
Merlin Cen. HP19: Ayle 5G 5
Merton Rd. HP27: Prin R 3F 33
Messenger Cl. HP21: Ayle 1C 12
Michaelis Rd. OX9: Tha 2C 24
Michaels M. HP19: Ayle 5E 5
Middle Farm Cl. OX39: Chin 6C 30
Middle Field HP22: West T 4H 13
Middle La. HP19: Ayle 4H 5
Middle Rd. HP21: Ayle 6D 6
Middle Way OX39: Chin 5B 30
Midhurst Cl. HP21: Ayle 2D 12
Midshires Bus. Pk. HP19: Ayle 4E 5
Miles Cl. HP21: Ayle 6C 6
Miles Ct. HP22: Bier 2D 6
Miles End HP21: Ayle 4H 5
Milford Pl. HP19: Ayle 5D 4
Millennium Point HP19: Ayle 4E 5
Millers Turn OX39: Chin 5B 30
Millers Way HP19: Ayle 5E 5
Mill La. HP22: West T 4H 13
  HP27: Mon R 5E 27
  OX39: Chin 5A 30
Mill Mead HP22: Wend 4B 22
Mill Mdw. HP19: Ayle 5F 5
Mill Path HP22: Wend 4B 22
Millstream HP22: West T 5H 13
Mill Stream Cl. HP27: Prin R 3E 33
Mill St. HP20: Ayle 4A 6
Mill Way HP20: Ayle 5G 5
Milton Gdns. HP27: Prin R 3E 33
Milton Rd. HP21: Ayle 1B 12
  HP22: Ast C 2F 15
Mimosa Ct. HP21: Ayle 1F 11
  (off Primrose Dr.)
Misbourne Cl. HP21: Ayle 4H 11
Missenden Rd. HP17: But X 1E 29
Mitcham Wlk. HP19: Ayle 3E 5
Mitchell Cl. OX9: Tha 2C 24
Moat, The HP18: Ayle 1B 4
Moat Cl. HP22: Wend 3B 22
Moat End HP22: Bier 1D 6
Moat's Cres. OX9: Tha 3E 25
Monet Pl. HP19: Ayle 3C 4
Monks Path HP19: Ayle 5E 5
  (off Hemp Hill)
MONKS RISBOROUGH 6G 27
Monks Risborough Station (Rail) 5F 27
Monmouth Cl. HP19: Ayle 3E 5
Montague St. HP21: Ayle 6H 5
Montesson Sq. OX9: Tha 3D 24
  (off Up. High St.)
Montrose Way OX9: Tha 3E 25
Moor End La. OX9: Tha 1E 25
Moorend La. OX9: Tha 2D 24
Moorhen Ct. HP19: Ayle 2A 6
Moorlands Ho. HP19: Ayle 5G 5
Moor Pk. HP22: Wend 2B 22
More Av. HP21: Ayle 6H 5
MORETON .5B 24
Moreton La. HP17: Bish 6F 11
  OX9: Tha 3C 24
Moreton Rd. OX9: More 4A 24
Morris Cl. OX9: Tha 3H 11
Mount Cl. HP22: Ast C 3F 15
Mt. Pleasant HP19: Ayle 4H 5
Mount St. HP20: Ayle 5H 5
Mount Way HP27: Prin R 2E 33
Mowbray Rd. HP20: Ayle 3H 5

Mullins Way HP19: Ayle 3C 4
Musgrave Rd. OX39: Chin 4D 30
Musket Path HP19: Ayle 1H 5

N

Napier Rd. HP19: Ayle 4C 4
Nappin Cl. HP19: Ayle 2D 4
Nappins Cl. HP18: Long C 3B 16
Narbeth Dr. HP20: Ayle 5D 6
Naseby Cl. OX9: Tha 2F 25
Nash Cl. HP21: Ayle 3C 12
NASH LEE .4E 21
Nash Lee End HP22: Wend 3H 21
Nash Lee La. HP22: Wend 3F 21
Nash Lee Rd. HP17: Terr 4E 21
  HP17: Wend 4E 21
  HP22: Wend 5A 22
Needlemakers HP18: Long C 2B 16
Nelson St. OX9: Tha 3D 24
Nelson Ter. OX9: Tha 5H 5
Nene Cl. HP21: Ayle 3G 11
NETHER WINCHENDON 2A 8
Nether Winchendon House 2A 8
Newburn Cl. OX9: Tha 4E 25
New Cl. Farm Rd. OX39: Hent 1C 30
New College Rd. HP19: Ayle 1G 5
Newell Cl. HP21: Ayle 1C 12
New Mdw. HP21: Ayle 1E 13
New Rd. HP17: Dint 5G 9
  HP22: Ast C, B'land 2E 15
  HP22: West T 6F 7
  HP27: Prin R 1F 33
New St. HP20: Ayle 4H 5
Neyland Dr. HP19: Ayle 2G 5
Nightingale Rd. HP21: Ayle 1A 12
  HP22: Wend 4B 22
Nocton Hall Dr. HP22: Halt 3E 23
Norfolk Ter. HP19: Ayle 4A 6
Normill Ter. HP22: Ast C 1A 14
North Dr. HP21: Ayle 2A 12
Nth. Eastern Rd. HP19: Ayle 3G 5
Northern Rd. HP19: Ayle 4G 5
Northfield Rd. HP20: Ayle 5D 6
  HP27: Prin R 1G 33
NORTH LEE 3D 20
North Lee La. HP22: Terr 2A 20
Northmill HP27: Prin R 2D 32
Nth. Mill Rd. HP27: Bled 6A 26
North St. OX9: Tha 2D 24
Northumberland Av. HP21: Ayle 1D 12
Norwood Cl. HP20: Ayle 3B 6
Nuffield Health Club
  Aylesbury 4E 5
Nugent Cl. HP19: Ayle 1H 5
Nursery Cl. HP21: Ayle 2G 11
Nuthatch HP19: Ayle 2B 6

O

Oak End Way OX39: Chin 6D 30
Oakfield Ho. HP21: Ayle 2B 12
  (off Hancock Cl.)
Oakfield Rd. HP20: Ayle 5C 6
Oak Grn. HP21: Ayle 6G 5
OAKLEY 6C 30
Oakley La. OX39: Chin 5B 30
Oakley Rd. OX39: Chin 6B 30
Oak Rd. HP27: Prin R 2G 33
Oat Cl. HP21: Ayle 4G 11
Oddley La. HP27: Saun 5A 32
Odeon Cinema
  Aylesbury 5A 6
Ogilvie Cl. HP22: Halt 3E 23
O'Grady Way HP19: Ayle 2E 5
Old Brewery Cl. HP21: Ayle 6A 6
Old Burrs HP21: Ayle 4H 11
Old Chapel Cl. HP17: Lit K 6A 20
Old Forge Gdns. HP22: Bier 1E 7
Oldhams Mdw. HP20: Ayle 3B 6
Old Manor Cl. HP27: Ask 4G 27
Old Mill Cl. HP17: Hadd 3G 17
Old Orchard OX39: Hent 1E 31
Old Orchards HP22: Bier 2C 6
Old Plough Cl. HP18: Che 1C 16
Old Risborough Rd. HP22: Sto M 1C 20
Old Sawmill Pl. OX39: Chin 5D 30
Old School Cl. HP22: Halt 6C 14
Old Stoke Rd. HP21: Ayle 1H 11
Old Tring Rd. HP22: Halt 4C 22
Old Union Way OX9: Tha 2C 24
Old Windmill Way HP18: Long C 2A 16

Oliffe Cl. HP20: Ayle 2H 5
Oliffe Way HP20: Ayle 2H 5
Olivier Way HP20: Ayle 5C 6
Onslow Dr. OX9: Tha 2E 15
Orchard, The HP22: Ast C 2E 15
   HP22: Halt 1C 22
Orchard Cl. HP20: Ayle 2B 6
   HP22: Sto M 6D 12
   HP22: Wend 3A 22
   HP27: Longw 4B 26
   OX9: Tha .3E 25
Orchard Ct. HP21: Ayle 1B 12
   (off Wendover Rd.)
Orchard Dr. HP22: Ast C 2E 15
Orchard Pl. HP27: Mon R 6G 27
Orchards, The HP17: Sto 2A 10
Orchard Way HP20: Ayle 3B 6
   OX39: Chin 5C 30
Ormesby Cl. HP21: Ayle 2C 12
Ormond Rd. OX9: Tha 2E 25
Orwell Cl. HP21: Ayle 3H 11
Orwell Dr. HP21: Ayle 3H 11
Osier Way HP20: Ayle 5B 6
Osprey, The HP19: Ayle 1A 6
Osprey Wlk. HP19: Ayle 1A 6
   (off The Osprey)
Ossulbury La. HP19: W'don 1G 5
Otway Cl. HP21: Ayle 4A 12
Oulton Cl. HP21: Ayle 2C 12
Overstrand HP22: Ast C 2E 15
Overton Dr. OX9: Tha 2F 25
Owen Pl. HP19: Ayle 4G 5
Owl Cl. HP19: Ayle 2B 6
OWLSWICK 2B 26
Owlswick La. HP27: Owls 3C 26
Oxford Rd. HP17: Dint, Hart, Sto, Upt 2A 10
   HP19: Ayle 6F 5
   HP20: Ayle 6F 5
   HP21: Ayle 6F 5
   OX9: Tha .3A 24
Oxpen HP18: Ayle 1B 4
Oxyard HP18: Ayle 1B 4

P

Paddock, The HP21: Ayle 6E 7
Paddock Cl. HP19: Ayle 4D 4
Paddocks, The HP17: Hadd 4G 17
   HP22: Wend 4B 22
PADDOCKS BMI CLINIC 1G 33
Padstow Cl. HP19: Ayle 4B 6
Pakenham Cl. HP19: Ayle 5D 4
Palfreyman St. HP19: Ayle 4A 12
Palmer Av. HP19: Ayle 4G 5
Paradise Orchard HP18: Ayle 1B 4
Park Ct. OX9: Tha 3E 25
Parker Wlk. HP19: Ayle 2H 5
Parkfield Ri. HP27: Prin R 3F 33
Park Mdw. HP27: Prin R 2E 33
Park St. HP20: Ayle 4A 6
   HP27: Prin R 2F 33
   OX9: Tha .3D 24
Park St. Ind. Est. HP20: Ayle 4B 6
Park Ter. OX9: Tha 4E 25
Park Vw. HP22: Ast C 3E 15
   OX39: Syde 2A 30
Parliament Rd. OX9: Tha 2D 24
Parmiter Cl. HP19: Ayle 5F 5
Parrin Dr. HP22: Halt 3E 23
Parrot Cl. HP21: Ayle 1F 11
Parsley Cl. HP22: Ast C 2C 14
Parslow Cl. HP21: Ayle 4H 11
Parslow Ct. HP21: Ayle 4H 11
   (off Sheridan Cl.)
Parson's Fee HP20: Ayle 5H 5
Parsons La. HP22: Bier 2D 6
Parton Cl. HP22: Wend 4A 22
Parton Rd. HP20: Ayle 5D 6
Partridge Way HP19: Ayle 2B 6
Pastures, The HP20: Ayle 3D 6
Paterson Rd. HP21: Ayle 6G 5
Patrick Way HP21: Ayle 2C 12
Pavers Cl. HP21: Ayle 5C 6
Pavilion Cl. HP20: Ayle 5C 6
Pavilion Gdns. HP22: Ast C 3E 15
Peacock La. HP19: W'don 1F 5
Pearce Cl. HP21: Ayle 3A 12
Pearce Ct. OX9: Tha 3D 24
Pearce Way OX9: Tha 4F 25
Pearson Cl. HP19: Ayle 1F 11
Peascroft HP18: Long C 3B 16
Pebble La. HP20: Ayle 1H 5
Pecks Farm Cl. HP22: Bier 1E 7

Peel Ct. HP27: Prin R 1F 33
Pegasus Way HP17: Hadd 3E 17
Peggs La. HP22: B'laud 2F 15
Pelham Rd. OX9: Tha 2F 25
Pemberton Cl. HP21: Ayle 2B 12
Pembroke Rd. HP20: Ayle 4B 6
Penfold HP22: West T 5H 13
Penley Cl. OX39: Chin 5B 30
Pennefather Ct. HP21: Ayle 6A 6
Pennings, The HP22: Wend 4B 22
Pennington Pl. OX9: Tha 2F 25
Penn Rd. HP21: Ayle 6H 5
Penrith Way HP21: Ayle 6D 6
Pentland Rd. HP21: Ayle 1B 12
Perch Mdw. HP22: Halt 1B 22
Peregrine HP19: Ayle 2A 6
Perry La. HP27: Bled 1H 31
Perry St. HP22: Wend 4A 22
Petersfield HP22: Sto M 4E 13
Peters La.
   HP27: Par H, Whit, Mon R 6H 27
Petronel Rd. HP19: Ayle 1H 5
Pevensey Cl. HP21: Ayle 2D 12
Peveril Cl. HP21: Ayle 2D 12
Philips Rd. HP19: Ayle 5E 5
Phipps Cl. HP20: Ayle 3C 6
Phoenix Cl. HP19: Ayle 4F 25
   (off Cotmore Gdns.)
Picasso Pl. HP19: Ayle 3D 4
Pickenfield OX9: Tha 4F 25
Picts La. HP27: Prin R 4D 32
Pike Corner HP21: Ayle 2E 13
Pilgrims Cl. HP27: Mon R 6F 27
Pine St. HP19: Ayle 4D 4
Pink Hill HP27: Par H 5H 33
Pink Rd. HP27: L Grn, Par H 6H 33
Pintail Cl. HP19: Ayle 1A 6
Pipit Gdns. HP19: Ayle 1A 6
   (off Fieldfare)
Pipit Wlk. HP19: Ayle 1A 6
Pippin Rd. HP18: Ayle 6B 4
Pitcher Wlk. HP19: Ayle 6E 5
   (off Fairford Leys Way)
PITCH GREEN .1H 31
Pitters Piece HP18: Long C 2A 16
Pitts Cl. HP22: Sto M 4E 13
Pixie Rd. HP18: Ayle 6A 4
Place Farm Way HP27: Mon R 5F 27
Players Theatre, The 3D 24
Playford Ct. OX9: Tha 3D 24
Pleasaunce, The HP22: Ast C 2E 15
Pleck La. OX39: King B 6A 30
Plested Ct. HP22: Sto M 5E 13
Plough Cl. HP21: Ayle 4A 12
Plough End HP22: Bier 2D 6
Plough Orchards HP22: West T 4H 13
Plover, The HP19: Ayle 1A 6
Plover Wlk. HP19: Ayle 1A 6
   (off The Plover)
Pluto Way HP19: W'don 1H 5
Plym Cl. HP21: Ayle 2G 11
Poets Chase HP21: Ayle 1B 12
Polish Av. HP22: Halt 1E 23
Pondecroft HP18: Ayle 1B 4
Pony Field, The HP22: West T 6F 13
Poole Cl. HP21: Ayle 3A 12
Popes Acre HP17: Hadd 4F 17
Pope Way HP21: Ayle 3A 12
Poplar Cl. HP20: Ayle 3C 6
Poplar Rd. HP20: Ayle 3C 6
Poplars, The HP22: Wend 4C 22
Poplars Cl. HP17: Sto 2A 10
Poppy Rd. HP27: Prin R 3E 33
Portal Rd. HP22: Halt 3D 22
Portman M. HP19: Ayle 5D 4
Portway HP17: Sto 3C 10
Portway HP17: Sto 2C 10
Potash Cl. HP17: Hadd 4F 17
Pottery Cl. HP19: Ayle 6E 5
Pottery Ct. HP19: Ayle 6E 5
   (off Pottery Cl.)
Pound St. HP22: Wend 5B 22
Prebendal Av. HP19: Ayle 1G 11
Prebendal Cl. HP20: Ayle 5H 5
Prebendal Ct. HP20: Ayle 5H 5
   (off Oxford Rd.)
PREBENDAL FARM 6G 5
Prebendal Ho. HP20: Ayle 5H 5
   (off Prebendal Cl.)
Premus HP19: Ayle 4E 5
Prestwold HP19: Ayle 6E 5
Prestwood Ho. HP19: Ayle 6E 5
   (off Prestwold Way)
Priest End OX9: Tha 2C 24

Primrose Ct. HP21: Ayle 1F 11
   (off Primrose Dr.)
Primrose Dr. HP21: Ayle 1F 11
Prince Rupert Dr. HP19: Ayle, W'don 1G 5
PRINCES ESTATE 2D 32
Princes Pl. HP27: Prin R 3F 33
PRINCES RISBOROUGH 1F 33
Princes Risborough Golf Course 6D 32
Princes Risborough Station (Rail) 3D 32
Prince's Rd. HP21: Ayle 5A 6
Princess Mary Dr. HP22: Halt 3D 22
Printers End HP19: Ayle 5F 5
Printers Piece HP17: Hadd 3G 17
Priory Cl. HP19: Ayle 3G 5
Priory Cres. HP19: Ayle 3G 5
Prothero Cl. HP21: Ayle 3A 12
Puffin Way HP19: Ayle 2B 6
Pump La. OX9: Tha 3D 24
Purbeck Cl. HP21: Ayle 2D 12
Purnell Wlk. HP19: W'don 1G 5
Purssell Pl. HP27: Prin R 6F 27
Putlowes Dr. HP18: Fleet M 1A 4
Putlowes Rd. HP18: Fleet M 1A 4
Putman Cl. OX9: Tha 3F 25
Putnams Dr. HP22: Ast C 2D 14
Puttenham Rd. HP23: Wils 1G 15
Pymcombe Cl. HP27: Prin R 6F 27
Pym Wlk. OX9: Tha 2D 24

Q

Quakers Mead HP22: West T 4H 13
Quakers Mede HP17: Hadd 3G 17
QUARRENDON 3E 5
Quarrendon Av. HP19: Ayle 3F 5
Quarry Cl. HP18: Long C 2A 16
Queens Cl. OX9: Tha 1D 24
Queensgate HP19: Ayle 5E 5
Queens Mead HP21: Ayle 6E 7
Queen's Pk. HP21: Ayle 5B 6
Queens Pk. Arts Cen. 5B 6
Queens Rd. HP27: Prin R 1G 33
   OX9: Tha .4E 25
Queen St. HP20: Ayle 5C 6
Quilters Way HP22: Sto M 1F 21

R

Rabans Cl. HP19: Ayle 3C 4
Rabans La. HP19: Ayle 4C 4
Racquets Fitness Cen.
   Thame 2D 24
Radnor End HP20: Ayle 3A 6
Railway St. HP20: Ayle 5A 6
Rainborough Gdns. HP20: Ayle 3A 6
Rake Way HP21: Ayle 4H 11
Ramworth Way HP21: Ayle 1C 12
Rannal Dr. OX39: Chin 5C 30
Raven Cl. HP19: Ayle 2B 6
Ravensbourne Rd. HP21: Ayle 4H 11
Ravensmead OX39: Chin 5D 30
Read Dr. HP22: Bier 1E 7
Read Ho. HP19: Ayle 6E 5
   (off Horton Cl.)
Reading Cl. HP19: Ayle 2E 5
Rectory Cl. HP27: Prin R 2F 33
Rectory Mdw. OX39: Chin 4D 30
Red Admiral St. HP19: W'don 1F 5
Redcliffe Wlk. HP19: Ayle 3F 5
Reddings Cl. HP22: Wend 3B 22
Rede Cl. HP19: W'don 1G 5
Red Kite Rd. OX39: Chin 6D 30
Redland Way HP21: Ayle 2C 12
Red Lion La. HP27: Longw 5B 26
Redwing HP19: Ayle 2A 6
Redwood Dr. HP21: Ayle 6A 6
Reflexions Health & Leisure 2H 5
Regency Ct. HP19: Ayle 6D 6
Regent Pk. HP27: Prin R 2D 32
Regent Rd. HP21: Ayle 6D 6
Rembrandt End HP19: Ayle 3D 4
Retreat, The HP27: Prin R 1F 33
Reynold Dr. HP20: Ayle 3C 6
Richmond Rd. HP20: Ayle 5E 7
Rickard Cl. HP21: Ayle 4H 11
Rickford's Hill HP20: Ayle 5H 5
Rickman Wlk. HP19: Ayle 6E 5
   (off Woodford Cl.)
Riders Way OX39: Chin 5C 30
Ridgebarn La. HP18: Cudd 3D 8
Ridge Cl. HP21: Ayle 4H 11
Ridge Way HP18: Long C 4D 16

Ridgeway Ct. HP20: Ayle 4A **6**
   (off Stirling Av.)
Ridgeway Meads HP27: Bled 1H **31**
Rifle Range Rd. HP17: Gt Kim 4A **28**
Riley Cl. HP20: Ayle 5G **5**
Rimmington Way HP19: Ayle 4F **5**
Ringlet Way HP19: W'don 1G **5**
Ringstead Way HP21: Ayle 2B **12**
Ripon Ho. HP21: Ayle 1B **12**
Ripon St. HP20: Ayle 5H **5**
Risborough Rd.
  HP17: Gt Kim, Lit K, Terr 4A **28**
   (not continuous)
  HP22: Sto M, Terr 6D **12**
Risborough Springs Swimming & Fitness Cen.
  . . . . .1E **33**
Rivets Cl. HP21: Ayle 1A **12**
Rixons Mdw. HP19: Ayle 6E **5**
Roald Dahl Gallery 5H **5**
   (in Buckinghamshire County Mus.)
Roald Dahl Ho. HP19: Ayle 5G **5**
Roberts Dr. HP19: Ayle 3H **5**
Roberts Rd. HP17: Hadd 3G **17**
Roberts Way HP21: Ayle 1F **11**
Robin Cl. HP19: Ayle 2B **6**
Robinson Cl. HP19: Ayle 2D **4**
Robins Platt OX39: Chin 5B **30**
Roblin Cl. HP21: Ayle 3A **12**
Rochester Pl. HP19: Ayle 5F **5**
Rodnall Cl. HP19: W'don 1H **5**
Rogue Racing
  Aylesbury 5B **6**
Roman Way HP19: Ayle 5F **5**
Romney Rd. HP21: Ayle 3A **12**
Rooks La. OX9: Tha 3D **24**
Rose Av. HP19: Ayle 3G **5**
Rosebery Rd. HP22: Ast C 2E **15**
Rosemary La. HP17: Hadd 2G **17**
Rosemead HP22: Halt 6E **15**
Rosemoor M. HP19: Ayle 5D **4**
Rothesay Cl. HP20: Ayle 4A **6**
Rothschild Av. HP22: Ast C 2E **15**
Rothschild Ho. HP19: Ayle 5G **5**
Roundhead Dr. OX9: Tha 1D **24**
Round Hill HP17: Sto 2B **10**
Roundhill Ct. HP17: Hadd 1E **17**
Rowan Cl. HP21: Ayle 3A **12**
Rowborough Rd. HP22: Halt 2D **22**
Rowland Way HP19: Ayle 6F **5**
Rowsham Rd. HP22: Bier 1E **7**
Roxwell Path HP20: Ayle 3B **6**
   (off Elmhurst Rd.)
ROYAL BUCKINGHAMSHIRE HOSPITAL . . .4H **5**
Royal Mead HP17: Terr 5E **21**
Rubens Cl. HP19: Ayle 3D **4**
Rudds La. HP17: Hadd 2G **17**
Run Furrow HP17: Hadd 2G **17**
Rupert Way OX9: Tha 2E **25**
Rushall Rd. OX9: Tha 2E **25**
Ruskin Way HP20: Ayle 3H **5**
Russell Av. HP21: Ayle 1G **11**
Russett St. HP18: Ayle 6B **4**
Rutherford Rd. HP21: Ayle 3A **12**
Rutland Path HP19: Ayle 4G **5**
Ryans Path HP19: W'don 1G **5**
Rycote La. OX9: Tha 4A **24**
Rye Cl. HP21: Ayle 3H **11**

S

St Agnes Ga. HP22: Wend 4A **22**
St Andrews Ct. OX9: Tha 3D **24**
St Andrew's Rd. OX39: Chin 6C **30**
St Andrews Way HP19: Ayle 4G **5**
St Andrews Way Ind. Est. HP19: Ayle 4G **5**
St Anne's Cl. HP22: Wend 4B **22**
St Anne's Rd. HP19: Ayle 5F **5**
St Anthony's Cl. HP19: Ayle 5F **5**
St Catherine's Ct. HP19: Ayle 5F **5**
St Dunstans Cl. HP27: Mon R 5G **27**
St Edmund's Cl. HP19: Ayle 5F **5**
St Hilda's Ct. HP19: Ayle 5F **5**
St James Way HP22: Bier 2D **6**
St Johns Dr. HP17: Sto 3A **10**
St John's Rd. HP20: Ayle 4A **6**
St John's St. HP20: Ayle 4A **6**
St Mark's Rd. HP19: Ayle 6G **5**
St Mary's Row HP20: Ayle 5H **5**
   (off St Mary's Sq.)
St Mary's Sq. HP20: Ayle 5H **5**
St Michaels Cl. HP22: Halt 1C **22**
St Peter's Av. HP19: Ayle 2G **5**
St Teresas Cl. HP27: Prin R 1F **33**

St Tiggywinkles Wildlife Hospital 5H **17**
Salisbury Cl. HP27: Prin R 2G **33**
Sandhill Way HP19: Ayle 5E **5**
Sandpiper HP19: Ayle 1A **6**
Sandpit La. HP27: Bled 2A **32**
Sandy La. HP18: Long C 3A **16**
Saturn Pathway HP18: Ayle 6B **4**
Saunders Pl. HP19: Ayle 6E **5**
SAUNDERTON 5D **32**
Savernake Rd. HP19: Ayle 2G **5**
Sawmill Rd. HP27: Longw 4B **26**
Scaldwell Pl. HP21: Ayle 3B **12**
Scarlett Av. HP22: Halt 3E **23**
School App. HP22: West T 4H **13**
School La. HP17: Dint 5H **9**
  HP18: Che 1C **16**
  HP22: West T .5G **13**
Scott End HP19: Ayle 3D **4**
Seabrook Ho. Cl. HP20: Ayle 4A **6**
Seabrook Ter. HP19: Ayle 3F **5**
   (off Coventon Rd.)
Seaton Dr. HP21: Ayle 3H **11**
Sedgemoor Dr. OX9: Tha 2E **25**
SEDRUP 4D **10**
Sedrup La. HP17: Hart 3D **10**
Selkirk Dr. HP19: Ayle 3H **5**
Selwyn Cl. HP21: Ayle 1D **12**
Serpentine, The HP19: Ayle 5G **5**
Seven Acres HP18: Long C 2A **16**
  OX9: Tha 3E **25**
Sewell Cl. HP19: Ayle 3D **4**
Sewell's La. OX39: Syde 5A **30**
Seymour Bus. Pk. OX39: Chin 5D **30**
Shaftesbury Ho. HP21: Ayle 6E **7**
Shakespeare Way HP20: Ayle 5C **6**
Shambles, The OX9: Tha 3D **24**
   (off Cornmarket)
Sharman Beer Ct. OX9: Tha 3C **24**
Sharp Cl. HP21: Ayle 2A **12**
Shaw Cl. HP20: Ayle 5C **6**
Shaw Ct. HP21: Ayle 4A **12**
Sheerstock HP17: Hadd 4E **17**
Sheerwater HP19: Ayle 1A **6**
Sheffield Dr. HP21: Ayle 1A **12**
Shelduck Cl. HP19: Ayle 2A **6**
Shepherd Cl. HP20: Ayle 3C **6**
Shereway HP19: Ayle 5F **5**
Sheridan Cl. HP21: Ayle 4H **11**
Sheriff Cl. HP21: Ayle 5F **5**
Shirley Cl. HP20: Ayle 3H **5**
SHOOTACRE CORNER 5E **33**
Shootacre La. HP27: Prin R 4D **32**
Shortborough Av. HP27: Prin R 6F **27**
Short Ditch HP17: Hadd 2G **17**
Shupp's La. HP18: Che 1C **16**
Siareys Cl. OX39: Chin 5C **30**
Sidney Ter. HP22: Wend 4B **22**
Silver Birch Way HP22: Sto M 3D **12**
Silverdale Cl. HP20: Ayle 4H **5**
Silver St. HP20: Ayle 5H **5**
Simmons Ct. HP21: Ayle 3A **12**
Simmons Way OX9: Tha 2D **24**
Simpson Pl. HP21: Ayle 2B **12**
Singleton Way HP19: Ayle 5E **5**
Sir Henry Lee Cres. HP18: Ayle 2B **4**
Skinner Rd. HP19: W'don 1F **5**
Skipper Cl. HP19: W'don 1G **5**
Skippon Way OX9: Tha 1D **24**
SKITTLE GREEN 1G **31**
Skittle Grn. HP27: Bled 1G **31**
Slade Hill HP19: Ayle 6E **5**
Slattenham Cl. HP19: Ayle 6F **5**
Slave Hill HP17: Hadd 4F **17**
Small White Path HP19: W'don 1G **5**
Smeaton Cl. HP19: Ayle 4D **4**
Smith Cl. HP20: Ayle 6D **6**
SMOKEY ROW 2A **28**
Somers Lees HP19: Ayle 5E **5**
Somerville Way HP19: Ayle 5F **5**
SOUTHCOURT 1F **11**
South End HP17: Hadd 4F **17**
Southern Rd. HP19: Ayle 4G **5**
  OX9: Tha 3C **24**
Southfield Rd. HP20: Ayle 5D **6**
  HP27: Prin R 2G **33**
South St. HP22: Wend 5B **22**
Southwold Cl. HP21: Ayle 1C **12**
Sovereign Ct. HP19: Ayle 2B **6**
Space Bus. Cen. HP19: Ayle 4E **5**
Sparrow Cl. HP19: Ayle 2B **6**
Spenser Rd. HP21: Ayle 1B **12**
Spicers Yd. HP17: Hadd 3G **17**
Spickett's La. HP18: Cudd 4B **8**
Spiert, The HP17: Sto 2B **10**

Spirit Health & Fitness Club 1G **13**
Spring Brook HP22: Ast C 3F **15**
Springfield Cl. HP21: Ayle 5G **5**
Springfield Gdns. OX39: Chin 4C **30**
Spring Path OX9: Tha 3C **24**
Springs Cl. HP17: Elle 1D **28**
Springs La. HP17: Elle 6D **20**
Spruce Rd. HP19: Ayle 5D **4**
Spurt St. HP18: Cudd 4B **8**
Square, The HP18: Long C 3A **16**
Stablebridge Rd. HP22: Ast C 3F **15**
Stable Rd. HP22: Halt 2D **22**
Staddle Stones HP27: Prin R 1F **33**
Stadium App. HP21: Ayle 3A **12**
Stafford Keep HP19: Ayle 5E **5**
Stanbridge Cl. HP17: Hadd 2G **17**
Stanbridge Rd.
  HP17: Hadd, King 2G **17**
Standfield Cl. HP19: Ayle 5E **5**
Standring Pl. HP20: Ayle 3B **6**
Stanhope Cl. HP22: Wend 2A **22**
Stanhope Rd. HP22: Wend 5C **6**
Stanton Ho. HP21: Ayle 6H **5**
   (off Coxhill Way)
Starling M. HP19: Ayle 5D **4**
Stars La. HP17: Dint 5G **9**
Station App. HP22: Wend 5B **22**
Station Rd. HP17: Hadd 4E **17**
  HP17: Lit K 1A **28**
  HP22: Sto M 6D **12**
  HP27: Prin R 3E **33**
  OX39: Chin 4C **30**
Station Way E. HP20: Ayle 6H **5**
Station Way W. HP20: Ayle 5H **5**
Station Yd. OX9: Tha 4E **25**
Staveley Cl. HP19: Ayle 1F **13**
Stephenson Cl. HP19: Ayle 5F **5**
Stirling Av. HP20: Ayle 4A **6**
Stock Ho. Pas. HP20: Ayle 5H **5**
   (off Silver St.)
Stocklake HP20: Ayle 4B **6**
   (not continuous)
Stocklake Ind. Est. HP20: Ayle 4B **6**
Stocklake Pk. Ind. Est. HP20: Ayle 4C **6**
Stockwell HP17: Hadd 3G **17**
Stockwell Furlong HP17: Hadd 3G **17**
Stockwell La. HP17: Mead 1B **26**
Stoke Farm La. HP21: Ayle 4A **12**
Stoke Leys Cl. HP21: Ayle 4A **12**
STOKE MANDEVILLE 5D **12**
Stoke Mandeville Stadium 2B **12**
STOKE MANDEVILLE HOSPITAL 3B **12**
Stoke Mandeville Station (Rail) 5E **13**
Stoke Rd. HP21: Ayle 1A **12**
Stokes Cft. HP17: Hadd 3G **17**
   (not continuous)
Stokes End HP17: Hadd 2G **17**
Stokes La. HP17: Hadd 2G **17**
STONE 2A **10**
Stonebridge Rd. HP19: Ayle 2F **5**
Stonechat HP19: Ayle 2A **6**
Stone Cft. HP17: Sto 2B **10**
Stonehaven Rd. HP19: Ayle 3F **5**
Stopps Orchard HP27: Mon R 6G **27**
Stork Cl. HP19: Ayle 2B **6**
Stour Cl. HP21: Ayle 3G **11**
Strafford Way OX9: Tha 3E **25**
Stratford Cl. HP22: Ast C 2C **14**
Stratford Dr. HP21: Ayle 1F **11**
Stratfords Way HP17: Hadd 3G **17**
Stratton Grn. HP21: Ayle 1D **12**
Stratton Path HP21: Ayle 1E **13**
Stratton Rd. HP27: Prin R 2E **33**
Streamside Wlk. HP21: Ayle 1G **11**
Stuart Way OX9: Tha 3E **25**
Stubble Hill HP19: Ayle 5E **5**
Stuchbury Cl. HP19: Ayle 5E **5**
Studland Cl. HP21: Ayle 2D **12**
Sulby Cl. HP21: Ayle 2G **11**
Summerleys Rd. HP27: Prin R 6C **26**
Summers Ho. HP21: Ayle 6H **5**
Sunnybrook Cl. HP22: Ast C 1D **14**
Sussex Cl. HP19: Ayle 2E **5**
Sutherland Wlk. HP21: Ayle 2B **12**
   (off Mellstock Rd.)
Swale Cl. HP21: Ayle 2G **11**
Swallow La. HP19: Ayle 5D **4**
  HP22: Sto M 5C **12**
Swan Cl. HP19: Ayle 2B **6**
Swan Hill HP18: Cudd 4B **8**
Swan M. HP22: Wend 4B **22**
Swann Rd. HP22: Halt 1C **22**
Swan Wlk. OX9: Tha 3D **24**
Swift Cl. HP19: Ayle 2B **6**

Sycamore Cl. HP18: Long C 3A 16
Sycamore Ct. HP19: Ayle 4H 5
Sycamore Dr. OX9: Tha 3B 24

T

Tacks La. HP17: Hadd 3F 17
Talbot Rd. HP22: Ast C 2E 15
Tamar Cl. HP21: Ayle 3G 11
Tamarisk Way HP22: Sto M 3E 13
Tavistock Wlk. HP20: Ayle 3A 6
(off Delamere Cl.)
Taylor Rd. HP21: Ayle 2H 11
Taylors La. HP23: St Leo 6H 23
Tedder Rd. HP22: Halt 4D 22
Tees Rd. HP21: Ayle 2G 11
Telford Cl. HP19: Ayle 4D 4
Templecroft Ter. HP17: Upt 3H 9
Temple Sq. HP20: Ayle 5H 5
Temple St. HP20: Ayle 5H 5
Tennyson Rd. HP21: Ayle 1B 12
TERRICK 4E 21
Terry Dr. HP19: Ayle 2G 5
Thackeray End HP19: Ayle 3D 4
THAME 3D 24
THAME COMMUNITY HOSPITAL 3E 25
Thame Leisure Cen. 3B 24
Thame Mus. .2C 24
Thame Pk. Bus. Cen.
  OX9: Tha .4E 25
Thame Pk. Rd. OX9: Tha 6D 24
Thame Rd. HP17: Hadd 3E 17
  HP18: Long C 4B 16
  HP21: Ayle 6G 5
  HP27: Longw 4A 26
  OX9: Tow .4H 25
  OX39: Chin 2A 30
Thame Rd. Sth. HP21: Ayle 1F 11
Thame Tennis Club 3F 25
The . . . .
  Names prefixed with 'The' for example
  'The Avenue' are indexed under the main
  name such as 'Avenue, The'
Thistle Ct. HP21: Ayle 2G 11
Thomson Cl. HP21: Ayle 1F 11
Thomson Wlk. HP21: Ayle 1F 11
(off Primrose Dr.)
Thorne Way HP20: Ayle 3B 6
  HP22: B'land 3G 15
Thorns Cl. HP27: Whit 6A 28
Thorns La. HP27: Whit 6H 27
Thornton Cres. HP22: Wend 4A 22
Thorpe Cl. HP21: Ayle 3C 12
Thrasher Rd. HP21: Ayle 1H 11
Thrush Cl. HP19: Ayle 2B 6
Tibbys La. HP18: Cudd 4B 8
Tichborne OX9: Tha 3E 25
Tillson Sq. HP21: Ayle 3B 12
Timber Way OX39: Chin 5C 30
Tindal Rd. HP20: Ayle 3A 6
Tinterne Cl. HP21: Ayle 1E 13
Titmus Rd. HP22: Halt 2E 23
Tiverton Cres. HP19: Ayle 2G 5
Todd Cl. HP21: Ayle 1F 11
Toll Bar Cnr. HP27: Longw 4B 26
Tolman Ct. HP21: Ayle 1F 11
Tompion Rd. HP19: Ayle 4D 4
Tompkins Cl. HP22: Ast C 3F 15
Torridge Rd. HP21: Ayle 3H 11
Tortoiseshell Rd. HP19: W'don 1G 5
Tourist Info. Cen.
  Aylesbury .5H 5
  Princes Risborough 2F 33
  Thame 3D 24
  Wendover .5C 22
Tower Ho. HP20: Ayle 5A 6
(off High St.)
Towersey Dr. OX9: Tha 4F 25
Towersey Rd. OX9: Tha 3F 25
Towersey Way HP21: Ayle 6G 5
(not continuous)
Town Farm Barns HP27: Prin R 2F 33
Town Farm Cl. OX9: Tha 3B 24
TOWNSEND .2G 17
Townsend HP17: Hadd 2G 17
Townsend Piece HP19: Ayle 4G 5
Townside HP17: Hadd 3F 17
Trebah Sq. HP19: Ayle 5D 4
Trenchard Av. HP22: Halt 3D 22
(not continuous)
Trenchard St. HP19: Ayle 5E 5
Treves Grn. HP21: Ayle 2A 12
Triangle Bus. Pk. OX9: Tha 1F 11

Tring Hill HP22: B'land 4H 15
  HP23: Tring 4H 15
Tring Rd. HP20: Ayle 5B 6
  HP22: Wend, Halt 5C 22
Trinity Ct. HP19: Ayle 4H 5
Trout Hollow HP27: Saun 5D 32
Tudor Ct. HP20: Ayle 5C 6
Turner Cl. HP20: Ayle 2B 6
Turner's Mdw. HP22: Ast C 1B 14
Turner Wlk. HP20: Ayle 2B 6
(off Turner Cl.)
Turnfurlong HP21: Ayle 6B 6
Turnfurlong La. HP21: Ayle 6B 6
Turnfurlong Row HP21: Ayle 1C 12
(off Turnfurlong La.)
Turnham Way HP19: Ayle 6F 5
Turnip Cl. HP18: Che 1C 16
Turnpike End HP21: Ayle 1B 12
Turnstone Way HP19: Ayle 2A 6
Turvey Cl. HP22: Ast C 2E 15
Turville Rd. HP21: Ayle 1F 13
Twitchell La. HP22: Ast C 2E 15
Tyneham Cl. HP21: Ayle 3D 12
Tyne Rd. HP21: Ayle 3H 11
Tythrop Way OX9: Tha 1D 24

U

Upende HP18: Ayle 1B 4
Up. Abbotts Hill HP19: Ayle 6E 5
Up. Church St. HP18: Cudd 4B 8
Upper Field OX39: Chin 6C 30
UPPER HARTWELL 2B 10
Upper Hartwell HP17: Sto 1C 10
Up. High St. OX9: Tha 3D 24
Up. Hundreds Way HP20: Ayle 5A 6
Up. Icknield Way
  HP22: Ast C, Halt 1D 22
  HP27: Bled, Prin R, Saun 4G 31
  HP27: Whit, Prin R 3F 33
  OX39: Chin 6D 30
UPTON 3H 9
Upton Rd. HP17: Dint, Upt 3H 9
Upton Ter. HP17: Upt 3H 9
Uxbridge Rd. HP22: Halt 3E 23

V

Vale Ho. HP19: Ayle 5G 5
Vale Ind. Centre, The HP19: Ayle 4G 5
Vale Pk. Dr. HP20: Ayle 5A 6
Vale Retail Pk. HP20: Ayle 5A 6
Vale Rd. HP20: Ayle 4A 6
Van Dieman's Rd. OX9: Tha 4D 24
Van Diemens Cl. OX39: Chin 4C 30
Vane Rd. OX9: Tha 3F 25
Verney Wlk. HP21: Ayle 1H 11
Verwood Rd. HP20: Ayle 3A 6
Vicarage Cl. HP22: Wend 4A 22
Vicarage Rd. HP21: Ayle 2H 11
Vickery Cl. HP21: Ayle 2A 12
Vickery Wlk. HP21: Ayle 2A 12
(off Vickery Cl.)
Victoria Mead OX9: Tha 4E 25
VICTORIA PARK 5C 6
Victoria St. HP20: Ayle 5B 6
Victory Rd. HP22: Wend 4B 22
Villiers Bldgs. HP20: Ayle 5H 5
(off Buckingham St.)
Vincent Rd. HP19: Ayle 2E 5
Vinetrees HP22: Wend 5B 22
Vineyards, The HP27: Bled 1G 31
Viney La. HP19: Ayle 5D 4
Viridian Sq. HP21: Ayle 6A 6
Viscount Cl. HP20: Ayle 3B 6

W

Waddesdon Grn. HP21: Ayle 3A 12
(off Winterton Dr.)
Wainhill OX39: Chin 3E 31
Wainwrights HP18: Long C 3B 16
Waivers Way HP21: Ayle 3C 12
Walker Dr. OX9: Tha 4F 25
Walker Pl. HP21: Ayle 2A 12
Walkers Rd. HP27: Longw 4B 26
Wallace End HP21: Ayle 1C 12
Wallbridge Cl. HP19: Ayle 6F 5
Wall Brown Way HP19: W'don 1G 5
Walnut Cl. HP18: Long C 2A 16
  HP22: Sto M 5E 13

Walnut Cres. HP27: Longw 4B 26
Walnut Dr. HP22: Wend 3B 22
Walnut Tree Ct. HP22: Sto M 4E 13
Walnut Tree La. HP27: Longw 5B 26
WALTON 6A 6
WALTON COURT 2G 11
Walton Ct. Cen. HP21: Ayle 2G 11
Walton Dene HP21: Ayle 6B 6
Walton Grn. HP21: Ayle 6A 6
Walton Gro. HP21: Ayle 6A 6
Walton Ho. HP21: Ayle 2B 12
(off Hancock Cl.)
Walton Pl. HP22: West T 4H 13
Walton Rd. HP21: Ayle 6A 6
Walton St. HP20: Ayle 5H 5
  HP21: Ayle .6A 6
Walton Way HP21: Ayle 6C 6
Wapping HP18: Long C 3B 16
Warbler Cl. HP19: Ayle 5D 4
Wardens Path HP19: W'don 1G 5
Wardrobes La. HP27: Loos 6H 33
Warneford Av. HP22: Halt 4D 22
Warren, The HP18: Ayle 1B 4
Warren Cl. HP17: Sto 2A 10
Warwick Cl. HP22: Ast C 2E 15
Warwick Row HP20: Ayle 4C 6
Water La. HP17: Ford 2A 18
Waterlily HP19: Ayle 1A 6
WATERMEAD .1A 6
Watermead HP19: Ayle 2H 5
Watermeadow HP19: Ayle 2B 6
Water Mdw. Way HP22: Wend 3B 22
Watermill Way HP22: West T 5H 13
Waterperry M. HP19: Ayle 5D 4
Waterslade Pens HP17: Hadd 3E 17
Watts Green HP18: Che 1C 16
Waverley Wlk. HP20: Ayle 3H 5
Waxwing Cl. HP19: Ayle 2A 6
Webbs Mdw. HP19: Ayle 5E 5
Webster Cl. OX9: Tha 2D 24
Webster Rd. HP21: Ayle 1C 12
Wedgewood St. HP19: Ayle 5E 5
Weedon Ct. HP19: Ayle 3H 5
WEEDON HILL .1G 5
Weedon Rd. HP19: Ayle 3G 5
Weill Rd. HP21: Ayle 3C 12
Welbeck Av. HP21: Ayle 6F 7
Werner Ct. HP21: Ayle 3A 12
Wesley Cl. HP20: Ayle 3C 6
Westbury Ho. HP20: Ayle 4H 5
(off Silverdale Cl.)
WEST END 5G 13
West End HP22: West T 5G 13
West End Pl. HP22: West T 5G 13
Westfield HP21: Ayle 4A 12
Westfields HP27: Whit 1H 33
West La. HP27: Bled 1G 31
WESTLINGTON 6G 9
Westlington La. HP17: Dint 6G 9
Westlington Lea HP17: Dint 6G 9
Westmead HP27: Prin R 6F 27
Westminster Dr. HP21: Ayle 1B 12
Westmorland Av. HP21: Ayle 1D 12
Weston Ct. HP22: Ast C 2C 14
Weston Rd. HP22: Ast C, West T 4B 14
WESTON TURVILLE 5H 13
Weston Turville Golf Course 3G 13
Weston Turville Reservoir 1A 22
Weston Way HP22: Sto M 5C 13
Weston Way Ind. Est.
  HP22: Sto M 5C 12

West St. HP19: Ayle 4H 5
Westwood Wlk. HP20: Ayle 3B 6
(off Hilton Av.)
Whaddon Chase HP19: Ayle 3G 5
Wharf Cl. HP22: Wend 4B 22
Wharf Rd. HP22: Wend 4B 22
Wharf Row HP22: B'land 3H 15
Wharton Ho. HP20: Ayle 4H 5
(off Silverdale Cl.)
Wheat Cl. HP21: Ayle 4A 12
Wheeler Cl. HP20: Ayle 5D 6
Wheelers End OX39: Chin 5C 30
Wheelwright Rd. HP27: Longw 4B 26
Wheelwrights HP22: West T 4H 13
Whinchat HP19: Ayle 2A 6
Whiskin La. HP21: Ayle 3B 12
Whitebeam Cl. HP22: Sto M 4E 13
Whitechurch Cl. HP17: Sto 2A 10
White Cres. HP22: Halt 2D 22
White Cross Rd. HP17: Hadd 4F 17
Whitehall St. HP20: Ayle 5H 5
White Hart La. HP17: Hadd 4G 17
Whitehead Way HP21: Ayle 1A 12
Whitehill La. HP19: Ayle 4H 5
White Horse M. OX9: Tha 3D 24
WHITELEAF 6H 27
Whiteleaf Cross 6A 28
Whiteleaf Golf Course 6A 28
Whiteleaf Hill Nature Reserve 6A 28
Whitethorn Cl. HP21: Ayle 3H 11
Whiteleaf Way HP27: Whit 6H 27
Whitethorn Cl. HP22: Sto M 1C 20
White Vw. HP20: Ayle 3B 6
Whitley Ct. HP21: Ayle 3A 12
Whittingham Av. HP22: Halt 3D 22
Whittle Rd. OX9: Tha 3F 25
Wickham Cl. HP20: Ayle 3A 6
Widdowson Pl. HP21: Ayle 2A 12
Wigan's La. HP27: Bled R 6A 32
Wigmore Ct. HP19: Ayle 3E 5
Wigmore Rd. HP19: Ayle 3E 5
William Burt Cl. HP22: West T 6H 13
William Harding Cl. HP21: Ayle 6A 6
William Hill Dr. HP22: Bier 1E 7
Williams Cl. HP19: Ayle 4H 5
Williams Way HP27: Longw 5B 26

Willis Rd. HP17: Hadd 4G 17
Willmott Cl. HP19: Ayle 1H 5
Willowbank Ter. HP21: Ayle 5A 6
Willowbrook HP22: Wend 2B 22
Willow Ct. HP19: Ayle 3E 5
HP21: Ayle 1G 11
Willow End HP22: West T 5H 13
Willow Ga. HP18: Che 1C 16
Willow Herb HP19: Ayle 1A 6
Willow Ho. HP20: Ayle 4H 5
(off Silverdale Cl.)
Willowmead HP17: Hart 2D 10
Willow Ri. HP17: Hadd 2G 17
Willow Rd. HP19: Ayle 4H 5
OX9: Tha .2D 24
OX39: Chin 5C 30
Willows, The HP27: Longw 5C 26
Willow Way HP27: Prin R 2E 33
Winchendon Rd. HP18: Che 1C 16
Winchester Ho. HP21: Ayle 1B 12
(off Bishops Wlk.)
Windermere Cl. HP21: Ayle 1D 12
Windmill Cl. HP19: Ayle 5F 5
OX9: Tow .4H 25
Windmill Hill HP27: Prin R 3F 33
Windmill Rd. HP17: Hadd 3F 17
OX9: Tha .4D 24
OX9: Tow .4H 25
Windrush Ct. HP21: Ayle 3H 11
Windsor Hill HP27: Prin R 6G 27
Windsor Rd. HP21: Ayle 6C 6
Wingate Wlk. HP20: Ayle 5C 6
Winston M. HP18: Ayle 6B 4
Winterton Dr. HP21: Ayle 4A 12
Wirethorn Furlong HP17: Hadd 3E 17
Witcham HP22: Wend 5B 22
Witham Way HP21: Ayle 3G 11
Wixon Path HP19: Ayle 5E 5
Woodbine Cl. HP27: Longw 6C 26
Woodfield Rd. HP27: Prin R 2G 33
Woodford Cl. HP19: Ayle 6E 5
Woodlands HP17: Hadd 3G 17
HP27: Prin R 2F 33
Woodmans Cft. HP19: Ayle 5E 5

Woods Pl. HP22: Wend 5B 22
Woodstock Cl. HP21: Ayle 1D 12
Woodville OX39: Chin 6C 30
Woodway HP27: Loos, Prin R 5F 33
Woodways HP17: Hadd 3G 17
Wood White Path HP19: W'don 1F 5
Woollerton Cl. HP27: Prin R 1F 33
Woollerton Cres. HP22: Wend 4C 22
Wootton La. HP17: Dint 6G 9
Worcester St. HP18: Ayle 6A 4
Wordsworth Wlk. HP21: Ayle 1B 12
(off Keats Cl.)
WORLD'S END .2H 21
World's End La. HP22: West T 5G 13
Wotton Path HP21: Ayle 4A 12
(off Kynaston Av.)
Wren Path HP19: Ayle 5D 4
(off Spruce Rd.)
Wroughton Rd. HP22: Halt 3E 23
Wycliffe End HP21: Ayle 5G 5
Wycombe Cl. HP21: Ayle 3D 12
Wycombe Rd. HP27: Prin R, Saun 3E 33
Wye Cl. HP21: Ayle 2G 11
Wykeham Ga. HP17: Hadd 4F 17
Wykeham Pk. OX9: Tha 3E 25
Wykeham Path HP19: Ayle 2H 5
Wykeham Ri. OX39: Chin 5D 30
Wykeham Way HP17: Hadd 3F 17
Wymering Rd. HP21: Ayle 1E 13
Wynford Grn. HP17: Ayle 1B 12
Wynne Jones Bus. Cen. HP21: Ayle 5B 6
Wyre Cl. HP17: Hadd 4G 17

Y

Yardley Grn. HP20: Ayle 3A 6
(off Hilton Av.)
Yeates Cl. OX9: Tha 2D 24
Yew Tree Cl. HP22: Sto M 6C 12
Yolsum Cl. HP17: Hadd 3E 17
Yorke Cl. HP22: Ast C 2E 15
York Pl. HP21: Ayle 6H 5
Youens Dr. OX9: Tha 4E 25
Young Cl. HP21: Ayle 1C 12

The representation on the maps of a road, track or footpath is no evidence of the existence of a right of way.

The Grid on this map is the National Grid taken from Ordnance Survey® mapping with the permission of the Controller of Her Majesty's Stationery Office.

Copyright of Geographers' A-Z Map Company Ltd.

No reproduction by any method whatsoever of any part of this publication is permitted without the prior consent of the copyright owners.

SAFETY CAMERA INFORMATION

PocketGPSWorld.com's CamerAlert is a self-contained speed and red light camera warning system for SatNavs and Android or Apple iOS smartphones/tablets. Visit www.cameralert.co.uk to download.

Safety camera locations are publicised by the Safer Roads Partnership which operates them in order to encourage drivers to comply with speed limits at these sites. It is the driver's absolute responsibility to be aware of and to adhere to speed limits at all times.

By showing this safety camera information it is the intention of Geographers' A-Z Map Company Ltd., to encourage safe driving and greater awareness of speed limits and vehicle speed. Data accurate at time of printing.